Societal Learning and Change

How Governments, Business and Civil Society are Creating Solutions to Complex Multi-Stakeholder Problems

Steve Waddell works as a researcher–
consultant–educator, with a focus on issues
and opportunities that require large systems
change. Often this change involves creating
business–government–civil society
collaborations or networks; these may be local,
national or global. Steve is founder and
Executive Director of the Global Action
Network Net (www.gan-net), which focuses on
building capacity of, and knowledge about,
Global Action Networks. He also is Senior
Associate at Strategic Clarity (www.strategic-
clarity.org) and the Institute for Strategic
Clarity, an adjunct faculty member innovative
executive management programme he founded
at Boston College, and an Associate of the
Collaborative Learning and Innovation group of
Simon Fraser University's Center for
Sustainable Community Development.

SOCIETAL LEARNING AND CHANGE

How Governments, Business and Civil Society
are Creating Solutions
to Complex Multi-Stakeholder Problems

STEVE WADDELL

Greenleaf
PUBLISHING

2 0 0 5

© 2005 Greenleaf Publishing Ltd

Published by Greenleaf Publishing Limited
Aizlewood's Mill
Nursery Street
Sheffield S3 8GG
UK
www.greenleaf-publishing.com

Printed on paper made from at least 75% post-consumer waste
using TCF and ECF bleaching.
Printed in Great Britain by William Clowes Ltd, Beccles, Suffolk.
Cover by LaliAbril.com.

British Library Cataloguing in Publication Data:
    A catalogue record for this book is available from the British Library.

Hardback: ISBN 1 874719 88 8
Paperback: ISBN 1 874719 93 4

Contents

Acknowledgements

A number of people and organisations have been particularly helpful to me in developing this book and the marvellous cases. I would like to thank in particular Severyn Bruyn who was far in the avant garde of social economy insights and a great teacher; and for the cases I am particularly appreciative of L. David Brown, the Institute for Development Research, the United States Agency for International Development, and the Ford and MacArthur Foundations, Ann Svendsen and Cesar Ledesma. And of course thanks to all those who spent patient hours with me talking about their work.

Preface

This is both a big-picture and a little-picture book. It describes how to bring about change in response to big issues such as globalisation, sustainability and inequity. However, as the cases in the book describe, the changes can start anywhere—with a farmer in the Philippines, an employee in a multinational corporation or a government official. This book brings into focus the obscure patterns of a new unfolding world to help people become involved in creating it.

The heart of the book is eight very diverse cases of remarkable change—change of individuals, organisations and society. The diversity of the cases aims to make the change accessible to a broad range of readers. The lessons drawn from these cases provide guidance for readers to achieve their own aspirations for change.

The paradigm shift in response to economic globalisation and environmental crises is not simply something we have to do. It is something that we *are doing*. It is complicated work, but it is absolutely achievable. It is work that, as the cases demonstrate, engages people in diverse positions in society and with very different viewpoints. Being a leader in the paradigm shift does not require a leadership position—but it does require a self-image of being a leader. In the words of my colleague, Joe Raelin, it requires *leaderfulness*. Everyone acts as a leader.

Wherever you are, you can make a contribution to shifting the paradigm through a societal learning and change strategy. As this book suggests, the critical contribution is creating new relationships between people and organisations that traditionally would not interact but in fact have common interests. When these relationships become meaningful by addressing a problem or developing an opportunity, people begin to learn about each other and develop mutual appreciation and understanding.

Often this process is complicated and confusing. People do not use words in the same way even if they speak the same formal language; they do not learn or perceive the world the same way although they share a common culture; their organisations have diverse goals, resources and weaknesses that make working together problematic. However, it is these very differences that are the source of the value of working together. This book aims to facilitate working through differences to work together successfully. It identifies some of the differences as sources of tension and opportunity and describes the development processes of building relationships that can produce mutually rewarding innovation that was unimaginable at the start of the relationship.

Chapter 1 introduces the concept of societal learning and change by breaking it into its core components: society, learning and change. It suggests that the type of deep change needed in response to many of today's major issues requires change in individuals (ourselves), organisations and societies—and that to focus on only one of these will result in failure. It also emphasises the importance of understanding diversity, and proposes that there are three archetypes that are particularly important to respect.

Chapter 2 may not interest everyone. It is a look at the historic development of the concept of societal learning and change (SLC). The concept is presented as a response to the fundamental movement to increased individual, organisational and societal diversity, and the need for us to hold together as common humanity.

The next chapter contains the cases themselves. These include two global cases (which people can readily participate in wherever they are), two cases from North America and four from Southern or developing countries. Often innovation occurs at the periphery of centres of power, as people are more pressed to innovate given their meagre resources. These cases also cover a range of issues and industries, including forestry, agriculture, infrastructure and banking.

Chapter 4 takes a deeper look at what exactly has changed in the cases. In particular it focuses on the concept of 'organisational sectors'—familiarly described as business, government and non-governmental organisations. As the chapter describes, these three sectors are grounded in individual archetypes, and therefore it is critical to recognise that change must address the needs of both people and organisations.

The motivations and forces for change are presented in Chapter 5. These are levers to stimulate and promote deep change by not just framing change as being in the interests of individuals and organisations but by creating synergies among them so they can support each other in the change.

The process of change is described in more detail in Chapter 6. It is broken into three stages of development, and key questions to address are identified for each stage. In addition, six classic mistakes are described. In Chapter 7 the structures of the new arrangements are described. These are inter-organisational relationships, separated into four different types. In effect, these are new networks that cross many divides of interests and demographics.

The lessons from the cases are summarised in Chapter 8. There are nine that may be succinctly summarised as emphasising the importance of empathetic relationships. Chapter 9 in conclusion looks to SLC strategies as being of increasing significance, given the increasing complexity of challenges and opportunities. Four core principles for operating in the SLC world and their implications for both human development and production systems are described.

The case studies are core reading. However, readers should feel free to dip into different parts of the book, and start with what you find most interesting. The best way to learn is to follow your curiosity and passions!

Chapter 1
Responding to crisis and opportunity

Smart companies are recognizing that the most effective way to leverage change in our interdependent world is through common endeavor with others. (Charles O. Holliday Jr, Chairman and CEO, DuPont, Stephan Schmidheiny, Chairman Anova Holding AG, and Philip Watts, Chair, Committee of Managing Directors, Royal Dutch/Shell, authors of *Walking the Talk: The Business Case for Sustainable Development*).

[The business and community-based organisations involved in fair trade are] . . . capturing a willingness of the world to move forward. (Raul Hopkins, International Fund for Agriculture Development, interview with author, 2001).

The people behind these statements inhabit very different worlds. The first are major business leaders who are talking about a source of success of their organisations with respect to sustainability. The second quotation comes from a person who grew up in poverty in Peru, works for an inter-governmental agency to address poverty and is talking about the complicated work of fair trade. But both are describing critical elements of the profound society-wide innovation that is essential in order to address the major challenges that confront us. This innovation is reconstructing our world by creating an intricate network or web tying together diverse organisations into a new governance structure that is generating innovation and producing societal learning and change.

SLC (societal learning and change) is taking place when:

- The World Resources Institute and other civil society organisations around the world join together in The Access Initiative to work with governments to give life to a widely ratified United Nations accord that makes participation a primary ingredient in environmental decision-making.

- In Pittsburgh in the United States a bank and local community organisations, with supportive government legislation, find ways to provide loans on a scale that transforms a community's opportunities and yet makes market-rate returns.

- After years of pitched battles, major forest companies, environmentalists, small communities and indigenous peoples on the Pacific Coast of Canada create the Joint Solutions Project to develop their future together.

- The French multinational Ondeo (formerly Suez Lyonnaise des Eaux), the South African non-governmental organisation Mvula Trust, other local companies and communities work together to create sustainable water systems for the rural poor.

- In the Philippines the local subsidiary of the American food giant Dole Foods, local small farmers, a non-governmental organisation (NGO) and the government work together to provide rice for the finicky Japanese market.

- Companies and civil society organisations around the world join together in the GRI (Global Reporting Initiative) to develop and apply an economic–social–environmental reporting framework.

- Major corporations, government and community-based organisations in Bangalore, India, produce agriculture and food-processing innovation.

- The Madagascar government transfers responsibility for roads to Road Users' Associations—NGOs newly created with the support of the United States Agency for International Development.

SLC is about changing relationships in profound ways and producing innovation to address chronic problems and develop new opportunities. These are not just interpersonal relationships, but relationships between large sections of society. Both the depth and breadth of the learning and change that SLC encompasses are unusual. SLC initiatives develop the capacity of a society to do something that it could not do before; they do the same thing for participating organisations.

The realignment involves changing relationships between the core systems of society—economic, political and social represented respectively by business, government and civil society. The goals of the organisations involved are varied: increasing profits, addressing environmental degradation, increasing equity, developing new products and markets, community development . . . But SLC always involves bridging the differences between business, government and community-based organisations (CBOs: see Box 1.1 for definitions of CBOs and civil society). By working together voluntarily, each participating organisation achieves its own goals by changing its relationship with others to co-ordinate their actions and create synergies. SLC is driven both by each group's goal and by a vision of how to build society's capacity to achieve a jointly valued societal goal.

One grand example of SLC is the transformation of South Africa from an apartheid society. To create a racially integrated society requires substantial change in not just the racial complexion of business, but the ways business works with non-whites as employees and customers. Similar to the ending of slavery in the US, ending apartheid restructured the economics of production. For government the end of apartheid meant substantial change in policing and justice systems, and rewriting of the basic governing document—the constitution. And for civil society the change meant shifting from a position of adversary to partner with other parts of society. With all this change, social structures become more closely aligned with the desires of its citizens and its potential for improving their welfare is substantially enhanced.

Civil society is a term in common usage almost everywhere in the world except the United States. The root of the term dates to Greek and Roman times, when it was equated with the state and government organisations. Today the term is used in two ways. Some use it to describe the totality of society and the interactions of its components. In this book it refers to a group of organisations that are 'a domain parallel to, but separate from, the state—a realm where citizens associate according to their own interests and wishes' (Carothers 1999). In this usage, the interests of the state are understood to be distinct from citizens' interests, even though democratic institutions aim to bring them into alignment.

The primary interest of the state is to maintain law and order. That of civil society is the achievement of community justice. 'Community' in this sense refers to communities of interest that may or may not be geographic—a neighbourhood group is obviously geographic and formed around the neighbourhood's interest; Greenpeace is global and formed around the issue of the environment. Although they are often associated with progressive values such as participation, accountability and transparency, they are not always progressive—in fact, they are very often protective of traditional values. For example, the Ku Klux Klan is a civil society organisation.

Community-based organisations (CBOs) are sometimes referred to as the voluntary, third, or independent sector. CBOs are often associated with non-governmental organisations (NGOs)—for example, environmental and neighbourhood groups—but they also include unions and churches. In the United States CBOs are often referred to as 'non-profits', but this term is simply a legal attribute among other attributes that these organisations often (but not always) possess. Moreover, not all non-profits are CBOs. See Chapter 4 for more information.

Box 1.1 Community-based organisations and civil society

By being aware that an initiative is an SLC one, you can substantially enhance its potential for success. SLC provides you with a framework for addressing complexity within a peer-based culture. Frameworks such as corporate citizenship and social responsibility, public policy, community development and corporate citizenship, treat communities, government or business as a privileged centre. In contrast, the SLC framework is one that emphasises 'we're all in this together', that no organisation is privileged and that all are interdependent. With this simple recognition, important barriers to success are overcome and innovation can arise on a grand scale.

SLC is occurring around the world. The examples in Chapter 3 reflect this: one each in Canada, the United States, South Africa, the Philippines, Madagascar and India, while two are global.

As well as being geographically widespread, SLC is happening on a variety of scales and with a variety of targets. The American banking example is organised around community-level concerns; the forest company and the Philippine rice project focus on industries and products; the South African development concerns public infrastructure for water supply and sanitation; and two further cases are global change strategies.

Rather than thinking of stakeholders *vis-à-vis* an organisation, SLC initiatives are stakeholders *vis-à-vis* a jointly defined issue. Each of the examples involves multiple organisations that *own* the issue. Initiatives often begin with a particular organisation, but success is indicated by transforming them into initiatives that are owned by multiple stakeholders. For example, before becoming independent the global SLC example of the GRI was nurtured for five years as a project of the NGO CERES (Coalition for Environmentally Responsible Economies). During that period ownership was expanded to include hundreds of organisations which jointly own GRI.

The SLC framework provides a disciplined way to approach complex and large-scale change issues. Whatever the change target, SLC action must follow processes that many find onerous. Initiatives need to be clearly outcome-focused and accountable to objectives. Discipline is a critical part of success, but so is experimentation and visioning. You must not think of these potential dichotomies as being in conflict, but rather as different facets of the same diamond. Without an SLC mindset that encompasses paradoxes, ambiguity and learning, SLCs have consumed hundreds of millions of budgeted dollars and innumerable person-hours with poor or mediocre outcomes. Clear, quantitative goals supported by learning processes that build knowledge and capacity for success are critical ingredients.

People find SLC inspirational because it connects their personal highest aspirations to their work of achieving what their organisations value. The tension between the quest to express our highest individual aspirations and the need to do organisationally valued work is an important driving force in producing the important large-scale change and innovation associated with SLC. The SLC approach is about creating the world that we intimately sense is needed, wanted and possible. SLC work holds the design of our visions in creative tension with the reality of what is, and closing the gap.

Higher aspirations include the desire to create wealth more broadly, address sustainable development, see justice and equity, and bring about peace. These were present in all the examples, but so were other more mundane aims about profits and maintaining the support of participating organisations by addressing short-term needs. In comparison to plantation traditions in the Philippines example, small farmers and Dole Foods have developed an agreement that reflects enhanced approaches to worker safety, the environment, and financial equity. The agreement involves core production issues such as how they work together, what they will do for one another as parts of the production chain, and how profits will be divided.

People are also inspired by SLC because it provides a way to work through problems and develop opportunities that are enormously complex and on a scale that can be paralysing. Of course, SLC is complicated and difficult to undertake successfully but, despite its youth as a concept, important knowledge and tools are already developing. And the more that people develop SLC initiatives, the greater the number of tools and capacity.

The core ingredients: society, learning and change

The SLC framework builds on individual, group and organisational learning and change approaches. In fact, SLC *requires* individual, group and organisational learning processes, since SLC success involves development of new individual and organisational capacity. These learning and change traditions are deep and rich, and provide a good strategic base and toolkit for SLC. However, with SLC there is the important additional level of society and this level has its own unique challenges and requires distinctive tools, knowledge and action.

The SLC framework also builds on the idea that there are basically three different types of individuals and organisations in the world, and these form three different types of *organisational sectors* and *societal subsystems*. Together, these create the SLC change challenge matrix presented in Table 1.1 and further described in Chapter 4. To produce SLC requires successful action at all the levels from individual to societal, and in two or, more often, three of the systems. The challenges produced by deep interaction between these systems are key to generating the deep and broad type of change that is distinctive of SLC. Those challenges help reveal unrecognised assumptions and allow combining unusual resources from the distinct systems in innovative ways.

Societal	Political systems	Economic systems	Social systems
Sectoral	The state sector	The market sector	The social sector
Organisational	Government agencies	Businesses	Community-based organisations
Individual	Mentally centred	Physically centred	Emotionally centred

TABLE 1.1 The societal learning and change challenge matrix

Regardless of the change target—community, industry, infrastructure or global action fields—SLC involves working with many individuals and dozens to literally thousands of organisations that do not have historic connections. This reflects the maxim that successful change efforts engage those who will be part of the change in defining the change, rather than simply acting on them. In the case of SLC, this means significant change with organisations in at least two of the three societal subsystems and the way they relate to one another. The political subsystem comprises government and its agencies that focus on setting the rules of the game and enforcing them; another is the economic subsystem, which is made up of businesses focusing on wealth creation; and the third is civil society and its organisations, which focus on promotion of their sense of justice and community well-being. Participants in SLC initiatives must understand their relative positions within the societal systems—and their core logics—to be able to work together effectively.

Of course there can be large change within any one of these three subsystems with relatively minor repercussions on the others. For example, the reorganising and integrating of the entertainment–communications industries is having an enormous impact on the structure of our economic system, but much less effect on our social and political ones. Admittedly *intra*sectoral changes can be complicated, but SLC is much more complex because of the diversity of the organisations involved. SLC in the case of the Pittsburgh bank and community, for example, required interaction between the economic, social and political systems as seen by the collaborative actions of NGOs, government agencies and banks.

SLC goes beyond the traditional protest, advocacy and lobbying of business and civil society organisations. Rather than people in one group telling others that they must change, in SLC all parties accept responsibility for changing themselves and their own actions to address the focal issue. They get together as stakeholders in the issue to jointly innovate to produce the change.

For any particular issue or opportunity, a societal perspective may arise in two different ways. For those who have a broad understanding about societal relationships and its subsystems, it might be present from the beginning. However, usually a problem or opportunity does not initially look as though it will involve societal change. Much more often this perspective arises as people persistently work to address a problem or develop an opportunity. They gradually develop an understanding that the barriers to success involve one of the other three societal subsystems. This can lead to them giving up because of the scale and complexity, or making some tentative futile attempts to bring about change with the conclusion that 'nothing can be done', or to a sophisticated SLC strategy that meets the scale of the challenge.

The strategy can include a range of actions. Traditional lobbying of government is a relatively primitive example of an SLC strategy; more sophisticated instances deal with the question of how to combine distinct weaknesses and strengths inherent in the subsystems to optimise outcomes. In the South African example of creating water systems for the rural poor, the SLC strategy overcame several traditional weaknesses such as government red tape, businesses' inattentiveness to long-term impacts and communities' lack of capacity to develop water systems on their own. That case also brought together government's competence to create a supportive operating environment, businesses' technical production acumen and civil society's ability to build capacity in communities to take charge.

Often the discovery that an issue involves SLC is demonstrated through changes in the definition of a problem or opportunity. On many occasions this change in definition is itself a key goal. Redefining 'the problem' was a core part of the process behind the global SLC The Access Initiative (TAI). Rather than simply telling government and business what to do, NGOs realised that one barrier to addressing environmental concerns is that government and civil society do not know how to work together very well, and a solution requires working together in new ways to access each other's core competences.

Learning as an ongoing process, and a spirit of continual exploration and discovery are part of SLC initiatives. Learning is important because these initiatives are complicated, they require capacity-building since few people have experience with them, and they must develop new knowledge since SLC as a concept and its supportive tools and processes are still in an early stage of development.

Although evaluations and assessments are popular and constitute learning-related activities, on their own they can easily undermine the learning approach that is needed for an SLC. One reason is that evaluations are often deflating, 'error-seeking' processes rather than generative learning ones. In SLCs, error- and blame-seeking approaches can be particularly problematic for two reasons. One is that SLCs depend on numerous organisations working together voluntarily in a network rather than a hierarchy, and blaming can easily result in an organisation simply leaving the collaboration. Punishments for exit are few, and participants must be attracted to stay. Another problem with evaluations on their own is that, due to the different languages of the three systems, conversations are complicated and the potential for misunderstanding is great. In one SLC meeting a physical fight almost broke out over the different uses of the word 'goal', which business tends to associate with reward-related short-term performance outcomes and civil society uses more loosely to describe a range of acceptable medium- and long-term outcomes.

From individual and organisational learning we know that there are basically two learning approaches and both of these are useful in SLC initiatives. One is experience-based and draws from the past. David Kolb popularised this as a cycle of experience–reflect–conceptualise–plan (Kolb 1984) (see Fig. 1.1) and it has resulted in tools such as 'after action reviews'. 'Experiencing' refers to looking at what is happening, data gathering and information production. 'Reflecting' is thinking about what the data means and turning it into knowledge, often through a group discussion. 'Conceptualising' turns the reflection into ideas about what to do differently. And 'planning' is putting the new learning into a new action plan.

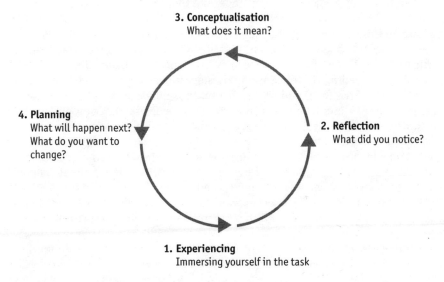

3. Conceptualisation
What does it mean?

4. Planning
What will happen next?
What do you want to change?

2. Reflection
What did you notice?

1. Experiencing
Immersing yourself in the task

FIGURE 1.1 The learning cycle

Source: www.css.edu/users/dswenson/web/pagemill/kolb.htm

This emphasises the importance of creating processes and routines that support these distinct stages of learning. It suggests that activities should be accompanied by documentation of what is actually done, and specific time be set aside to review it as a group. These reviews might be set on a calendar basis, or around a particular time in a project cycle. Learning histories can be a useful tool. In the Pittsburgh banking case, this process produced a 'live' document that recorded major decisions and milestones.

This learning approach is usefully grounded in what happened, but the past orientation has limitations. Future-oriented processes are particularly important in SLCs. Together these processes actively connect aspirations and work. Future-oriented learning is focused on possibilities rather than experiences. Planning tools such as scenario planning can be useful, and a whole set of such tools, sometimes described as 'large group/system interventions', is particularly appropriate for SLCs (Holman and Devane 1999).

Putting together the learning and the change parts of SLC is core SLC activity. Learning is happening all the time, but it is of negligible importance if it stays with a small group of individuals or in a little-read academic manuscript. SLC emphasises the value of connecting learning to change. Change is always happening all around us, but it usually feels as if it is happening to us and driven by an inexorable confusion of forces rather than as something that can be consciously guided. On a global level, this is the essential critique of opponents of globalisation, who sprang into public view with demonstrations against the World Trade Organisation at Seattle in 1999. Essentially they were saying that they had not been engaged in defining the direction of economic change, and that its design had been restricted to those with economic as opposed to social or political system concerns. This situation indicates that there was inadequate attention to the 'system boundaries'.

Defining system boundaries means identifying two change dimensions that are particularly important for SLC stakeholders in the action domain. One is the dimension of breadth. This dimension raises questions about the definition of the action domain (Trist 1983) and *who* is affected or could be usefully engaged by the change issue. As described earlier, this might be people and organisations associated with a community, an industry, a specific infrastructure or a global issue, as is common with environmental issues. In the Philippine case, Dole Foods did not traditionally involve small farmers and NGOs in its production; rather, its history is with company-owned plantations. However, land redistribution in the Philippines led the company to rethink the possibilities and bring into its action domain an NGO and small farmers. This reflects a characteristic SLC redefinition of the 'who', which is often critical for innovation. It also often involves creating a structure for traditionally ignored voices to be heard.

The other change dimension is one of depth. This is often classified into three categories: single-, double- and triple-loop learning (Argyris and Schon 1978; Nielsen 1996) paralleled with first-, second- and third-order change (Bartunek and Moch 1987). The 'loops' involve increasingly deep learning and reflection, and 'orders' are ever-deepening change.

First-order change involves change within the current rules of the game. For example, changing the quantities in a quota system describes a single-loop learning model of change. Something has changed in the operating environment—maybe an industry voice has become louder or imports have grown—and a change in the quota quantity results. The quota system and the way quantities are defined are accepted. The only variable is the number.

With second-order change, the basic decision-making framework remains the same although its structure changes. In the quota example this might mean applying quotas to an import that had never been subject to them before.

SLC always involves third-order change, in which the basic structure and decision-making framework are changed. To carry on with the quota example, third-order change would be reflected in throwing out the quota system altogether with the conclusion that it was no longer valid or that some other strategy would be more effective. This requires 're-visioning' future possibilities.

This re-visioning process is referred to as 'generative dialogue' (Jaworski *et al.* 2004; Scharmer 2001). Figure 1.2 illustrates the stages involved, moving from the bottom left quadrant, to bottom right, to upper right, ending in the upper left quadrant. It usually begins with 'talking nice', when people are simply civil to one another, and this moves into 'talking tough' where people state their positions and tell each other how they should change. This stage can lead to 'reflective dialogue' where parties move from advocacy into inquiry and from the past into imagining their individual futures. When the relationship develops a conversation about how they can all work together differently through innovation by creating a new whole, they have passed into generative dialogue.

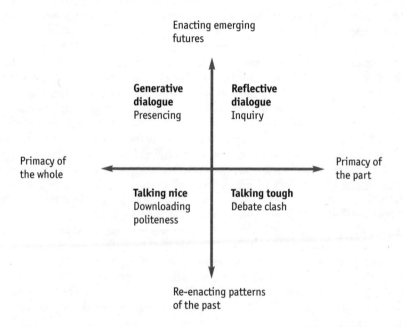

FIGURE 1.2 Four fields of conversation

Source: Scharmer 2001

SLC third-order change usually starts with government or civil society prodding. In the GRI example, the first move came with the formation of CERES by environmentalists such as the Sierra Club joining with shareholder activists aiming to change corporate behaviour by voting on resolutions at corporate annual meetings. From that base they developed relationships with corporations that led to a shared view that change was necessary at the societal level as well as the organisational level. Development of a more consistent, multi-stakeholder and widely used environmental reporting framework was identified as the vehicle to achieve this. This resulted in the GRI, whose mission is third-order change. In the bank example, the change began with NGO agitation, which produced legislative changes that in turn spurred some banks to participate in SLC strategies. In the forest example, the companies, environmentalists and communities became worn out from fighting and realised they had to do something different.

However, a potential SLC change can stall with a move by only one of the societal systems. In the TAI example, this occurred when nations signed an agreement in 1992 to make participatory practice a key factor in environmental decision-making. It was only ten years later with civil society action that global progress began. In the banking example, pressure from community activists led to new rules obliging the banks to supply information they had never provided before. New regulations required that banks report on their outreach activities with communities. For a long time, banks treated these demands simply as an additional second-order-change regulatory reporting burden (and many banks still do). However, in some instances, the right combination of people both in banks and in communities made something different happen, resulting in third-order change.

When SLC initiatives begin with a high level of conflict, as in the forests of Western Canada, triple-loop learning occurs after parties talk and listen to each other, and move into a process of learning that leads to innovation (Svendsen *et al.* 2003). Usually SLC starts with organisations taking adversarial positions that challenge the status quo. Parties merely state their positions and concerns. In the forest case, the companies and environmentalists battled for media coverage. When leaders of indigenous peoples came forward and pointed out that they had an interest (redefining the system boundaries), this helped people to start listening to one another and understanding each other's views. Combined with consumer protests, this resulted in movement into a learning mode. Companies signalled this movement with a commitment to phase out clear-cut logging, the most offensive part of their operations. The environmentalists for their part agreed to halt protests while shape was given to the so-called Joint Solutions Project, envisioned as a long-term framework for working together.

SLC initiatives do not have to begin with conflict—although they almost always start after the failure of less ambitious attempts. For example, the South African government had been trying to provide water for its rural citizens for some time. However, within months the new water systems would break down and people would go back to their traditional (often unsafe and distant) water supplies. Eventually, when civil society organisations were engaged, the community gained a sense of ownership of the water system and their capacity to maintain the system was developed.

These change processes are not quick. The banking example occurred over a period of 25 years, although during the first 20 years the parties simply repeatedly declared their views ('talking tough') while the government built a more supportive underlying framework for change with reflective inquiry about the problems. There is often a long incubation stage when parties wear themselves out with fighting or people become frustrated with the results of non-SLC strategies, and finally decide to do something differently. But even when parties decide to work together to do something there are many pitfalls. Even the best-organised efforts take three to five years to produce results of the type reflected in the original vision.

As we learn more about SLC and develop our tools and capacities, this process will shorten. However, most of the time saving will come from reduction in the unproductive declarative positioning stage and fumbling around with solutions designed within one sector and activities disconnected to learning. Change processes of the depth and breadth implied by SLC simply take time. But the mounting demands for complex change, particularly obvious with issues of sustainable development, show that we have no other choice than to press forward with SLC strategies.

References

Argyris, C., and D. Schon (1978) *Organizational Learning: A Theory of Action Perspective* (Reading, MA: Addison-Wesley).

Bartunek, J., and M. Moch (1987) 'First Order, Second Order and Third Order Change and Organization Development Interventions: A Cognitive Approach', *Journal of Applied Behavioral Science* 23: 483-500.

Carothers, T. (1999) 'Civil Society', *Foreign Affairs*, Winter 1999/2000: 18-25.

Holliday, C.O., Jr, S. Schmidheiny and P. Watts (2002) *Walking the Talk: The Business Case for Sustainable Development* (Sheffield, UK: Greenleaf Publishing).

Holman, P., and T. Devane (1999) *The Change Handbook: Group Methods for Shaping the Future* (San Francisco: Berrett-Koehler).

Jaworski, J., P. Senge, O. Scharmer and B.-S. Flowers (2004) *Presence: Human Purpose and the Field of the Future* (Cambridge, MA: Society for Organizational Learning).

Kolb, D.A. (1984) *Organizational Psychology: An Experiential Approach to Organizational Behavior* (Englewood Cliffs, NJ: Prentice Hall).

Nielsen, R.P. (1996) *The Politics of Ethics: Methods for Acting, Learning and Sometimes Fighting with Others in Addressing Ethical Problems in Organizational Life* (ed. R.E. Freeman; New York: Oxford University Press).

Scharmer, C.O. (2001) 'Self-Transcending Knowledge: Organizing around Emerging Realities', in D. Teece (ed.), *Managing Industrial Knowledge: Creation, Transfer, and Utilization* (Thousand Oaks, CA: Sage Publications).

Svendsen, A.C., M. Laberge and R.G. Boutilier (2003) *Five Stages of Stakeholder Engagement* (unpublished manuscript; Vancouver, BC).

Trist, E. (1983) 'Referent Organizations and the Development of Inter-Organizational Domains', *Human Relations* 36: 269-84.

Chapter 2
Where does the SLC concept come from?

SLC is a relatively new concept, although its roots are old. It draws from traditions that ask questions about what makes a society successful and what change processes will lead societies to be more successful. Naturally enough these questions have roots in the disciplines that dominate the three societal subsystems: law, political science and public administration in the political system; economics and business in the economic system; and psychology, anthropology and sociology in the social system. Each asks questions relating to societal change. However, the responses are often highly problematic because they are not integrated with the other subsystems. In systems thinking language, they do not consider the feedback loops (adverse reactions, unintended consequences) from the other subsystems because they treat their own focal system as self-contained and independent.

For example, economic solutions most often ignore political and social implications. The economic-system focus of the architects of globalisation has produced protests from the other systems. Economic-system architects have not sufficiently considered and understood the repercussions of their narrow focus on the social and political systems, such as inequality, erosion or downplaying of the role of government, and degradation of the environment. Nor have they considered the important political questions about power and participation of people in decisions that affect them.

The trend since the early 1980s has been to increasing power of the economic system. In terms of philosophy and principles, this was reflected in what is called 'The Washington Consensus'[1] (Williamson 1990, 2002). This was agreement among the major global economic–political actors—global business, the International Monetary Fund, the World Bank, the United States and eventually the World Trade Organisation—that solutions to the world's problems would be found by unleashing the energy of the market. Earlier with the rise of the welfare state during the Great Depression and after World War II, there was increasing power of the political system as a strategy to make societies more successful. Government became the guarantor of basic services and regulator of the economic system.

---

1   The term was used originally in 1989 and argued that the set of policy reforms that most of official Washington thought would be good for Latin American countries could be summarised in ten propositions.

This history shows a shift in emphasis between two of society's subsystems—the political and economic—as being the source of the type of change needed to make a society successful. A systems perspective emphasises the need for balance of power among them. The process that determines the appropriate balance is the fundamental dynamic behind negotiating the 'social contract'.

The sociology behind SLC

SLC fits into social change and development traditions of sociology. These describe the way social (individual, group, organisational and institutional) relationships restructure themselves in response to developments such as new technology and knowledge, environmental pressures and shifting ideologies and values (Chirot 1994; Jaffee 1990; McMichael 2000; Peet 1999; Vago 1999).

One of the most helpful theoretical traditions in sociology for understanding and developing SLC initiatives is societal evolution theory. This arises from one of the classic questions in sociology named (after the 17th-century English thinker) the 'Hobbesian problem of order'. What binds people together to form 'society' in the face of one key trend that is driving societal change and innovation, something social scientists call 'differentiation'?

As civilisation progresses, people tend to distinguish themselves from one another in increasingly specialised ways. This is most obvious in terms of specialisation of work. In contemporary society people rarely have the in-depth understanding about each other's work that people in agrarian societies traditionally possessed. But differentiation covers a whole range of qualities. Whereas communities used to be cohesive in terms of religious faiths, there is increasing mingling of different ones. At one time countries could be described as 'white' racially, but with migration and historic events such as slavery, this is less and less true. Countries used to be classified as 'Catholic', but such classifications today are more historic than reflective of church attendance today. New social identities such as those developed by gays and lesbians are becoming more prominent.

But if we increasingly identify ourselves as being different and even unique, what enables us to share the same community and world successfully rather than simply generating a growing babble of difference? There are, of course, some contrary forces such as economic globalisation which tend to extinguish some differences such as with European currencies transforming into the euro and with McDonald's becoming a global food phenomenon. Many of these forces have negative impacts such as the disappearance of cultures, languages and options for living, such as the elimination of nomadic lifestyles. SLC initiatives are arising as an increasingly important activity to both address the desire to offset some of these negative impacts and build bridges between the differences.

These issues about bridging differences (integration and differentiation) have been taken up by all the great sociologists. In the 19th century the German sociologist Tonnies popularised a view that there were basically two periods in human social development: pre-modern with traditional interpersonal family and community ties among people who knew one another (*Gemeinschaft*), and the modern (*Gesellschaft*) world dominated by ties that are utilitarian and based on external characteristics such as language (Tonnies 1963). Durkheim similarly used the terms 'organic' and 'inorganic' solidarity, and wrote about the impact of the division of labour and the resulting difficulty in people relating to each other (anomie) in comparison to when their work was similar (Durkheim 1966). Weber described our evolution into a society dominated by a work ethic, saving and rationalism that produced capitalism and ordered bureaucracies (Weber 1930). Marx distinguished between various phases of social evolution and focused on economic forces to distinguish between more numerous states of evolution, including feudal, capitalist, socialist and communist (Marx 1859/1973).

Marx's concept of the 'economic superstructure' as the key change agent evolved into socioeconomic development theory, which emphasised the role of the economy. Modern sociologists transformed classical ideas of class and societal change into a 'dynamic systems' view of the world. 'The most essential condition of successful dynamic analysis (of social change) is continual and systematic reference of every problem to the state of the *system as a whole*,' commented Talcott Parsons (1949; italics added). He identified four systems, each with a particular function, in a hierarchy of control. The most powerful integrating system was cultural, followed by the social system, personality system and behavioural organism (Parsons 1951). Unfortunately for people wanting to design societal change initiatives, this analysis is difficult to operationalise, in part because it mixed levels of analysis ranging from the environment to individuals.

Rudolph Steiner helped to create an operating framework for societal learning and change with the concept of 'threefolding'. Steiner said that society was comprised of three distinct 'spheres'. One is the economic sphere, which concerns production; a second is the sphere of civil rights, which refers to the political sphere of law-making, governance and definition of how people interact; and the third is the cultural sphere, which refers to free human spirit expression with thinking, morality and creativity (Perlas 2000; Steiner 1999).

This line of thinking was further developed by Amitai Etzioni, who looked at organisations from the perspective of distinct forms of power. He identified three types of organisations: the governmental type where power is coercive (police, laws, courts), the business type that depends on calculative and instrumental (financial payments) power to achieve its goals, and non-profits where power is normative and people act based on shared values (Etzioni 1961). In Chapter 4 these organisational types are expanded to create *organisational sectors* of the state, market and civil society which in turn represent the three critical societal systems— political, economic and social. This analysis can be combined with Parsons' view that different systems in society have different functions, in order to organise societal learning and change initiatives in a strategic way. The societal challenge of integration in the face of differentiation is answered in part by SLC initiatives that weave together these three different systems.

Societal learning and change is introduced

SLC aims to help operationalise these big theoretical perspectives about society and change, by better understanding the implications for individuals and organisations (businesses, governments, CBOs) and collections of them (organisational sectors, associations, networks, coalitions). If a critical issue requires addressing, or if we want to move the world in general in a direction of sustainability, what should we do? How can we organise ourselves and develop change?

In response to a Club of Rome report on learning, in 1980 a panel discussed the concept of 'societal learning'. The panel referred to the report as 'a first step towards a capacity study of societal learning' (Botkin *et al.* 1980). Most of the panel conceived of societal learning as a rather simplistic aggregation of individual learning and framed the challenge in terms of storing and accessing data in a comprehensive way. However, the panel pushed the boundary to encompass the concept as it is used here, by referring to a 1978 presentation by Ambassador Soedjatmoko of Indonesia (appointed rector of the United Nations [UN] University in 1980) who stressed the importance of the 'learning capacity of nations':

> The capacity of a nation—not just of its government, but of society as a whole—to adjust to rapidly changing techno-economic, socio-cultural and political changes, on a scale which makes it possible to speak of social transformation, very much depends on its collective capacity to generate, to ingest, to reach out for, and to utilise a vast amount of new and relevant information. This capacity for creative and innovative response to changing conditions and new challenges I would like to call the learning capacity of a nation. This capacity is obviously not limited to the cognitive level, but includes the attitudinal, institutional and organisational levels of society as well (Judge 1980).

The traditional literature on social and economic development was tied to the concept of societal learning by Anthony Judge, for a UN University Working Group. He urged a 'switch from interpreting actions in terms of their significance for development to their significance as learning'. He went on to underline the difference as being about the relationship between people during the processes, commenting that

> It is strange that 'development' is conventionally a process applied to, or undergone by 'others'—never by the 'developers', despite their well-documented limitations. It is acknowledged that good teachers succeed partly because their attitude is one of learning with, and from, the student—to the point that 'facilitator' is more appropriate than 'teacher'.

The Working Group advocated moving from the model of 'developing society' to 'learning society' and 'societal learning' distinguished by its ability to generate its own answers in a more inclusive sense (Judge 1982; see Box 2.1).

One of the next references to the concept of societal learning arose with Milbrath's *Envisioning a Sustainable Society*. He explains that an indicator of societal learning is 'when a dominant institution or practice is replaced by another' (Milbrath 1989: 89), and gives the example of slavery and its abolition. Easy sharing of information is critical to societal learning, and networks are seen as particularly

Often people use 'social' and 'societal' learning interchangeably. Milbrath uses the word 'social', but really means change in deep structures in the same way that 'societal' is used here. However, some people use the term 'social learning' to refer to the way an individual learns (Bandura 1986, 1997; Vygotsky 1978). The latter emphasise the role of observing and modelling the behaviours, attitudes and emotional reactions of others in individual learning processes.

Box 2.1 'Social' versus 'societal' learning

good vehicles for information dissemination. Milbrath emphasises the importance of networks that support holistic thinking and help connect parts of society that traditionally have been unassociated.

Building on individual learning and organisational learning traditions, Austrom and Lad observed: 'The emergence of new values in support of [inter-organisational] collaboration implies a societal learning process [as] . . . individuals and organisations begin to realise the relative advantages of working together as well as the necessary social skills' (Austrom and Lad 1989). The authors identify as critical to development of societal learning the emergence of new key 'logics' in terms of basic world-view, implicit logics and leading values.

Writing nearly a decade later, Brown and Fox defined societal learning as 'articulating new paradigms that can alter the perspectives, goals, and behaviors of social systems larger than particular organizations' (Brown and Fox 1998: 474). Societal learning is associated with outcomes of reshaped public awareness, and local political and societal contexts. Processes of accountability, transparency and participation are identified as particularly important for societal learning.

SLC has been investigated as a product of coalitions constructed across North–South (developed–developing) country divides (Brown 1998). Initiatives aiming to address problems by involving organisations from government, business and civil society are investigated, with the view that societal learning is something 'indicated by changes in [inter-organisational] arrangements that enable multiple organizational actors to understand and work together effectively' (Brown and Ashman 1998: 16). The authors identify as key to successful problem-solving across the sectors:

- The presence of social capital as with the presence of local institutions and intersectoral actors

- Decision-making processes that moderate conflict and ensure grass-roots participation

- Societal learning, which depends on (a) learning activities through programme learning, organisation learning and societal learning; and (b) catalyst roles—individuals who pressed for solutions when problems arose (Brown and Ashman 1998: 16)

SLC-related approaches

Rich sources of work relevant to SLC include international development, inter-organisational relationships, collaboration and business–society frameworks such as corporate citizenship and social responsibility. Some milestones deserve mention. Working in the tradition of social systems thinking, Ackoff gave his famous description of 'messes' (Ackoff 1974) to describe a social issue that involves unclear responsibility and jurisdiction and an intermingling of interests where no one is clearly responsible; this often describes SLC situations. Trist helped develop the concept of a 'problem domain' and 'referrant organization' (Trist 1983) that is connected to the concepts of 'system boundaries' and 'stakeholders' (Freeman 1984) in an organisation. The problem or issue domain is the field of people and organisations that are affected by, or could be affected by, the issue. When these domains are organised, particular organisations arise that represent distinct groupings of interests (stakeholders) and these are referrant organisations. SLC works best when these organisations are mature and can work together.

Coming from the inter-organisational relationship tradition, Brown introduced the concept of an 'under-organised' system to describe a situation where new relationships or institutions have to be created to turn a series of ad hoc actions by various people and organisations into a coherent system (Brown 1980, 1983). Barbara Gray was one of the first academics to focus on business–government–civil society relationships and developed the concept of collaboration and its relationship to shared vision (Gray 1981, 1989, 1990). Associated work with Donna Wood (Wood and Gray 1991) further developed the connection between practice and theory that placed negotiating as an important connecting activity.

The inter-system dynamic of collaborations led to the concept of bridging organisations (Brown 1991, 1993; Lawrence and Hardy 1999; Sharma *et al.* 1994; Westley and Vredenburg 1991), which 'span social gaps to mobilize cooperation among diverse stakeholders who cannot solve the problems by themselves' (Brown 1993: 381). The types of relationship stretched to include social partnerships (Waddock 1991), catalytic alliances (Waddock and Post 1995), the collaborative enterprise (Halal 2001) and the 'civil corporation' (Zadek 2001).

Of course there is also an extensive amount of work specifically on business and society relationships with the concepts of corporate social responsibility (Carroll 1999) and corporate citizenship (Andriof and McIntosh 2001; Waddock 2002). For civil society these relationships have often been associated with questions about community development and addressing environmental issues; for government these relationships are associated more with innovative approaches to creating and implementing public policy.

In the early 1990s a new stream of more conscious SLC-related work began with development agencies such as the Inter-American Development Fund, the United States Agency for International Development and later the World Bank. With the rise of the International Business Leaders Forum in London, important initiatives began with business and other organisations, which produced important practitioner-supporting concepts and tools (Nelson 1996, 1998; Nelson and Zadek 2000). By the beginning of the millennium, a good base was established for understanding business–government–civil society collaboration from various perspectives (Logan *et al.* 1997; Plummer and Waddell 2002; Regelbrugge 1997; Svendsen 1998; Waddell 1998, 2000; Waddock 2002; Zadek 2001; Zadek *et al.* 2001) and a large number of SLC initiatives, both local and global were under way.

References

Ackoff, R. (1974) *Redesigning the Future: A Systems Approach to Societal Problems* (New York: John Wiley).

Andriof, J., and M. McIntosh (2001) 'Introduction: What is Corporate Citizenship', in J. Andriof and M. McIntosh (eds.), *Perspectives on Corporate Citizenship* (Sheffield, UK: Greenleaf Publishing): 13-24.

Austrom, D., and L. Lad (1989) 'Issues Management Alliances: New Responses, New Values, and New Logics', *Research in Corporate Social Performance and Policy* 11: 233-55.

Bandura, A. (1986) *Social Foundations of Thought and Action* (Englewood Cliffs, NJ: Prentice Hall).

—— (1997) *Self-Efficacy: The Exercise of Control* (New York: WH Freeman).

Botkin, Ja.W., M. Malitza and M. Elmandjra (1980) *No Limits to Learning: Bridging the Human Gap. A Report to the Club of Rome* (New York: Pergamon Press).

Brown, L.D. (1980) 'Planned Change in Underorganized Systems', in T.G. Cummings (ed.), *Systems Theory for Organization Development* (Chichester, UK: John Wiley): 181-208.

—— (1983) *Managing Conflict at Organizational Interfaces* (Reading, MA: Addison-Wesley).

—— (1991) 'Bridging Organizations and Sustainable Development', *Human Relations* 44: 807-31.

—— (1993) 'Development Bridging Organizations and Strategic Management for Social Change', *Advances in Strategic Management* 9: 301-405.

—— (1998) 'Social Learning in South–North Coalitions: Constructing Knowledge Systems across Social Chasms.' *IDR Reports* 14.

—— and J. Fox (1998) 'Accountability within Transnational Coalitions', in L.D. Brown and J. Fox (eds.), *The Struggle for Accountability: The World Bank, NGOs and Grassroots Movements* (Cambridge, MA: The MIT Press).

Carroll, A.B. (1999) 'Corporate Social Responsibility: Evolution of a Definitional Construct', *Business and Society* 38: 268-95.

Chirot, D. (1994) *How Societies Change* (Thousand Oaks, CA: Pine Forge Press).

Durkheim, E. (1966) *On the Division of Labor in Society* (trans. G. Simpson; New York: The Free Press).

Etzioni, A. (1961) *A Comparative Analysis of Complex Organizations* (New York: The Free Press).

Freeman, R.E. (1984) *Strategic Management: A Stakeholder Approach* (Boston, MA: Pitman).

Gray, B. (1981) 'Fostering Collaboration among Organizations', in H. Maltzer and W.R. Nord (eds.), *Making Organizations Humane and Productive: A Manual for Practitioners* (New York: John Wiley).

—— (1989) *Collaborating: Finding Common Ground for Multiparty Problems* (San Francisco: Jossey-Bass).

—— (1990) 'Building Interorganizational Alliances: Planned Change in a Global Environment', *Research in Organizational Change and Development* 4: 129-66.

Halal, W.E. (2001) 'The Collaborative Enterprise: A Stakeholder Model Uniting Profitability and Responsibility', *Journal of Corporate Citizenship* 2 (Summer 2001): 27-42.

Jaffee, D. (1990) *Levels of Socio-economic Development Theory* (New York: Praeger).

Judge, A. (1980) 'Societal Learning and the Erosion of Collective Memory. A Critique of the Club of Rome Report: No Limits to Learning', paper presented at *Second World Symposium on International Documentation*, Brussels, Belgium.

—— (1982) 'Development as Discontinuous Societal Learning: Cyclic Transformation of the Global Answer Economy', in United Nations University: GPID Project (Integrative Working Group B), Colombo, Sri Lanka.

Lawrence, T.B., and C. Hardy (1999) 'Building Bridges for Refugees: Toward a Typology of Bridging Organizations', *Journal of Applied Behavioral Science* 35: 48-70.

Logan, D., R. Delwin and L. Regelbrugge (1997) *Global Corporate Citizenship: Rationale and Strategies* (Washington, DC: Hitachi Foundation).

Marx, K. (1859) 'A Contribution to the Critique of Political Economy', in H.G. Selsam, D. Goldway and H. Martell (eds.), *Dynamics of Social Change: A Reader in Marxist Social Science* (New York: International Publishers, 1973).

McMichael, P. (2000) *Development and Social Change* (Thousand Oaks, CA: Pine Forge Press).

Milbrath, L.W. (1989) *Envisioning a Sustainable Society: Learning Our Way Out* (Albany, NY: State University of New York).

Nelson, J. (1996) *Business as Partners in Development: Creating Wealth for Countries, Companies and Communities* (London: Prince of Wales Business Leaders Forum in collaboration with the World Bank and the United Nations Development Programme).

—— (1998) *Building Competitiveness in Communities: How World Class Companies are Creating Shareholder Value and Societal Value* (London: Prince of Wales Business Leaders Forum in collaboration with the World Bank and the United Nations Development Programme).

—— and Simon Zadek (2000) *Partnership Alchemy* (Copenhagen: The Copenhagen Center).

Parsons, T. (1949) 'Position and Prospects of Systematic Theory in Sociology', in T. Parsons, *Essays in Sociological Theory* (New York: The Free Press): 212-37.

—— (1951) *The Social System* (Glencoe, IL: The Free Press).

Peet, R. (1999) *Theories of Development* (New York: Guildford Press).

Perlas, N. (2000) *Shaping Globalization: Civil Society, Cultural Power and Threefolding* (Quezon City, Philippines: Center for Alternative Development Initiatives).

Plummer, J., and S. Waddell (2002) 'Building on the Assets of Potential Partners', in J. Plummer (ed.), *Focusing Partnerships: A Sourcebook for Municipal Capacity Building in Public–Private Partnerships* (London: Earthscan Publications).

Regelbrugge, L. (1997) 'Engaging Corporations in Strengthening Civil Society', in L.M. Fox and S.B. Shearer (eds.), *Sustaining Civil Society: Strategies for Resource Mobilization* (Washington, DC: CIVICUS): 211-47.

Sharma, S., H. Vredenburg and F. Westley (1994) 'Strategic Bridging: A Role for the Multinational Corporation in Third World Development', *Journal of Applied Behavioral Science* 30: 458-76.

Steiner, R. (1999) *Towards Social Renewal: Rethinking the Basis of Society* (trans. M. Barton; London: Rudolf Steiner Press).

Svendsen, A. (1998) *The Stakeholder Strategy* (San Francisco: Berrett-Koehler).

Tonnies, F. (1963) *Community and Society* (trans. C.P. Loomis; New York: Harper & Row).

Trist, E. (1983) 'Referent Organizations and the Development of Inter-Organizational Domains', *Human Relations* 36: 269-84.

Vago, S. (1999) *Social Change* (Upper Saddle River, NJ: Prentice Hall).

Vygotsky, L. (1978) *Mind in Society* (Cambridge, MA: The MIT Press).

Waddell, S. (1998) *A Strategic Framework for Explaining and Building Government–Business–Civil Society Collaboration* (Boston, MA: Institute for Development Research/MacArthur Foundation).

—— (2000) 'New Institutions for the Practice of Corporate Citizenship: Historical, Intersectoral, and Developmental Perspectives', *Business and Society Review*, Spring 2000: 107-26.

Waddock, S. (1991) 'A Typology of Social Partnership Organizations', *Administration and Society* 22: 380-415.

—— (2002) *Leading Corporate Citizens: Meeting the Business in Society Challenge* (New York: McGraw-Hill/Irwin).

—— and J. Post (1995) 'Catalytic Alliances for Social Problem Solving', *Human Relations* 48: 951-73.

Weber, M. (1930) *The Protestant Ethic and the Spirit of Capitalism* (London: Allen & Unwin).

Westley, F., and H. Vredenburg (1991) 'Strategic Bridging: The Collaboration between Environmentalists and Business in the Marketing of Green Products', *Journal of Applied Behavioral Science* 22: 65-90.

Williamson, J. (1990) 'What Washington Means by Policy Reform', in J. Williamson (ed.), *Latin American Adjustment: How Much Has Happened?* (Washington, DC: Institute for International Economics).

—— (2002) 'What Should the World Bank Think about the Washington Consensus?', *World Bank Research Observer* 15: 251-64.

Wood, D.J., and B. Gray (1991) 'Toward a Comprehensive Theory of Collaboration', *Journal of Applied Behavioral Science* 27: 139-62.

Zadek, S. (2001) *The Civil Corporation: The New Economy of Corporate Citizenship* (London: Earthscan Publications).

——, N. Hojensgard and P. Raynard (eds.) (2001) *Perspectives on the New Economy of Corporate Citizenship* (Copenhagen: The Copenhagen Center).

Chapter 3
The case studies

Amanz'abantu and water systems in South Africa

Author

Steve Waddell

Case type

Infrastructure development—water and sanitation

Location

Eastern Cape Province, South Africa

Sectoral context

South Africa has sophisticated government, business and civil society structures. However, their distribution and those who engage in them are still influenced by the history of apartheid. With the ending of apartheid, civil society was weakened as many of its leaders moved to government.

Major participants

- Mvula Trust
- Suez Lyonnaise des Eaux
- Group Five Civils Ltd (Group Five)
- Ninham Shand East Ltd in association with Fongoqa Skade Toyi & Associates Close Corporation
- Set Point Industrial Technology Ltd in association with Khulani Ground Water Consultants Ltd
- National Department of Water Affairs and Forestry

Societal goal

- Development of sustainable water systems

Civil society goal

- Provision of water for the poor
- Construction with community benefits
- Control of the water system by its users

Government goal

- Provision of basic water services that is demand-driven and community-based
- User pays (for maintenance)
- Environmental integrity
- Cost-effectiveness
- Developing capacity of local communities
- Provision of broad community benefits
- Transition from apartheid

Business goal

- Design and construction of the infrastructure
- Role in long-term maintenance
- A competitive rate of profit

SLC product

Providing safe water for the world's people is a challenge that has stymied many significant efforts. As a consequence, about two billion people still lack safe water. Past approaches in developing countries dominated by government were notoriously slow and financially non-sustaining; those by civil society faced problems of scale and speed of delivery; and those by business have not met challenges of sustainability and cost-effectiveness. In effect, months after government- or business-led construction was completed, systems were often unusable since there was inadequate maintenance. A new intersectoral approach overcomes these shortcomings by building systems with high community capacity and commitment to maintain them.

Description

The very complex apartheid history of South Africa, which created a race-based first-world country within a third-world one, is reflected in many activities in the country. The turning points in the struggle against apartheid came in 1990 with the release of Nelson Mandela from prison and in 1994 with the first election when all adult citizens were able to vote. Over this time a series of sophisticated interventions brought together government (white), business (white) and civil society (mainly non-white) to build relationships and create a collective vision of the future.

Water services were a priority of the new government, and by 1996 it had sufficiently developed ideas for a new approach to issue a request for proposals (RfP). The government issued four build–operate–train–transfer (BOTT) requests for proposals, one for each of four provinces. This included the Eastern Cape province where about 61% of its eight million inhabitants are in poor rural communities. Six million are in need of provision of water services, although the province is considered water-rich.

Respondents to the RfP for the Eastern Cape included a consortium of construction and design companies called Amanz'abantu (AA) and an NGO called Mvula Trust ('the Trust'; 'Mvula'). The government urged both parties to combine forces—it was not confident that the Trust could deliver on the scale needed, and it was not confident that AA would be able to carry out the community and institutional and social development (ISD) activities the government wanted.

As leader of the AA bid, Oliver Ives followed up this suggestion by contacting Mvula's managing director, Piers Cross. The two men were already familiar with one another. Mvula expressed both strong interest and reservations about working with the for-profit companies in a consortium. The Trust was anxious to play the role of representative of social development interests and the communities, but how could it ensure that the group took ISD concerns seriously? Mvula would only be one voice and a small non-profit organisation among some large for-profit companies.

The parties worked out an agreement to address these concerns and combine forces. Mvula was made responsible for providing ISD with veto power over hiring for some key positions. Also, Mvula was given a seat on the AA board. However, to avoid conflict of interest with its primary goal to support the communities' interests, it chose not to be a shareholder and therefore would not gain financially from its board position. Another wrinkle stipulated by the South African government meant that non-white contractors would become increasingly large shareholders over time.

In the South African BOTT system both physical and social infrastructure are built to avoid the problems of earlier approaches. The community must be fully engaged in planning and building the infrastructure, community commitment to contribute to it financially must be nurtured, and community capacity to maintain the water works developed. Although the government takes the lead in organising the approach and the private sector is involved in building it, the community must be able to take charge.

The first AA project

The village of Mgwangqa is high up in the barren hills facing the East Indian Ocean in the Eastern Cape Province of South Africa. It has approximately 90 households, totalling about 500 inhabitants. Most of the residents have moved here from nearby farms and other areas. The vast majority of the population is unemployed and pension benefits are the major income source. A 2 km dirt road leads to the main road and the nearest town, Peddie, is 8 km away.

Traditionally the villagers depended for their water supply on collecting rainwater and using dammed water shared with animals. Given that the region has about 600 mm of rain a year, the villagers were better off than many rural South African communities. However, the rain does not fall evenly through the year and health problems arise from the use of these traditional water sources, including scabies among children, diarrhoea among all ages, and food poisoning.

In the BOTT approach, the government approves AA projects on an individual basis. The politicians were anxious to show some outcomes of their work, and the Peddie scheme was targeted as a key project. Work on the scheme had been off and on during the past decade, there was pressure from citizens to see it completed, and the construction aspects could be undertaken more rapidly than a brand-new project. In October 1997 the Department of Water Affairs and Forestry (DWAF) gave its approval to the $6 million Peddie Regional Water Supply Scheme to bring water to standpipes within 200 m of households. Construction commenced on 1 November 1997.

The development process at Peddie is presented in Figure 3.1. ISD was first in and last out together with operations and management (O&M; which involves starting up the facility and building villagers' capacity to maintain it). One key development point is the commissioning certificate when the water first flows; a second is the transfer certificate when ownership of the system is transferred from the national government to the local community.

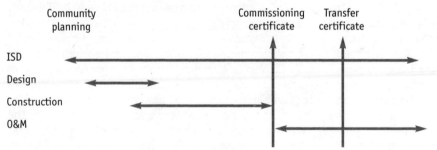

FIGURE 3.1 The project cycle

The community and institutional development parallelled the physical construction. The initial focus for construction was on the bulk infrastructure (i.e. the water works, bulk pipelines and reservoirs) with the village piping following six months later. Mvula pressed ahead with its own work to develop village water committees (VWCs) in four villages by organising five workshops and information meetings. These sessions were highly popular, with over 50% of the residents participating with a balance of men and women. Each village established a VWC with 18 people, and they formed a joint project steering committee (PSC) of eight.

A labour desk was formed in each village, with a seven-member VWC labour subcommittee, for the purpose of hiring local residents to assist in construction. They were paid on a piecework basis—for example, per cubic metre of earth removed. The committee members received payment for attending meetings.

In the BOTT approach the VWCs and PSCs are developed as important transparent decision-making bodies. Although DWAF is the source of funds, it also has a client role since it approves budgets, hires local labour and ensures that the community is committed to decisions made. In the case of Peddie, 352 people were hired for contracts of about three months' duration and earned R1,900,000 (about $300,000). For many it was their first paying job. Although a labour-intensive approach results in about 10–20% higher costs, it is accepted as part of a local development strategy. Local subcontractors are given strong preference, and AA works with them to improve their own business skills as well as to fulfil their contracts. The VWCs also take responsibility for ensuring each household makes the required R10 (about $1.50) contribution to the project. (By the end of the Peddie project, about 98% of households had paid.)

Workshops continue after forming the committees, developing members' leadership and meeting skills. These leaders explain to their fellow villagers the key steps in the projects as a *masakane* strategy—meaning 'let's build together'. For community members workshops include 'Learning to value water'.

In AA the Trust plays a key role in building the local government capacity to play a meaningful part in the development. The VWCs and PSC are nominally in charge of project planning decisions and their ability to carry out this function must be built up. In addition, the Trust has a major responsibility for creating a sense of ownership by local villagers in the project, including a commitment to pay for a portion of the infrastructure development and for maintenance fees. A third role for the Trust is to facilitate the hiring of villagers by AA contractors as construction labour. On top of this, the Trust has a leading role in supporting new economic development initiatives within the community as part of the government's integrated development strategy. AA also must contract a percentage of its work from historically disadvantaged communities' (HDCs—in effect, non-white) businesses.

The villagers of Mgwangqa obtained access to running water when the President arrived on an election tour and turned the tap. By the end of April 2000, AA in the Eastern Cape had completed R283.5 million (about $50 million) worth of work; 2000/2001 through 2003/2004 it had contracted for another R450 million. Of this, nearly R8 million went directly to HDCs. Through access ranging from provision of hand pumps to standpipe water systems, by the end of April 2000 over half a million people had been provided with a new water source.

Financially AA met its profit goals and also provided an 8% discount for the government on its originally contracted rates. This resulted from increased efficiencies, a clearer understanding of customer requirements and an improved definition of the scope of work. The government obtained a further 1.25% discount for early payment.

SLC features

Integrating social and physical infrastructure development

Usually social infrastructure questions about whether people have the skills and institutions to manage their own affairs are ignored when developing physical infrastructure, or treated paternalistically through a centralised government answer, or at best considered an 'add-on' or side activity. The BOTT approach recognises the need to integrate their development with physical infrastructure construction.

Changing race relations through contracts

Affirmative action through preferential contracting by government to ensure that women, minorities and the traditionally marginalised are given fair opportunities is not new. However, the South African approach is much more integrated by considering issues such as skills transfer by pairing advantaged and disadvantaged companies, and wealth transfer by ensuring the HDC have an increasing ownership share of AA.

Putting the traditionally marginalised in charge

The villagers of Mgwangqa have a profile that fits classic definitions of marginalised, with little education or power. But rather than building the water system for them, as passive recipients, the BOTT strategy takes advantage of the water development scheme to also build their capacity to be in charge and become active decision-makers and citizens.

Companies redefining their product

The for-profit companies in AA had always approached their work within the context of building physical water infrastructure. To achieve success, they had to reframe their work within the context of building a sustainable water system.

Bringing a non-shareholder into a for-profit consortium

Bringing Mvula into AA as a non-shareholder was a novel move which helped Mvula maintain its integrity (and value to AA) while being an 'insider'. This theoretical relationship was difficult to operationalise, however. The Trust felt itself excluded or at least insufficiently included in some decisions, such as the amount of AA profits that should be returned to shareholders.

Introducing informal market members to the formal market

Most of the villagers had no experience as 'employees' before. By contracting work to them they became acquainted with the expectations and benefits associated with the formal market economy.

Transforming forestry in Canada

Author

Ann Svendsen

Executive Director for Collaboration and Innovation at
Simon Fraser University in Vancouver, Canada

Case type

Industry—forestry

Location

Pacific Coast of Canada

Sectoral context

Canada is often presented as being halfway between the European corporatist model of strong labour–government–business collaboration and that of the United States where the sectors are more separate but the economic sector is dominant. Forestry companies are large and sophisticated. The government is deeply involved in forestry since forests are government- rather than privately owned. Labour was the principal civil society organisation to be involved in forestry historically. This case is marked by the entry of environmental organisations and the First Nations (indigenous peoples) into the issue in a large way.

Major participants

- MacMillan Bloedel (MB) Forest Company
- Coalition of Environmental Groups
- International Woodworkers Association
- Provincial government (Ministry of Environment, Ministry of Forests)
- Nuu-Chah-Nulth First Nations
- Communities of Uclulet and Tofino

Societal goal

- Create a sustainable approach to forestry

Civil society goal

- Ensure conservation of old-growth forests
- Employee safety
- Spur development of more sustainable approach to forestry/logging

Government goal

- Resolution of unresolved land claims and aboriginal title issues of First Nations
- Sustained tax revenues from forest-sector employment and related economic development
- Resolution of the resource conflicts

Business goal

- Employee safety
- Profitability
- Ensure a good reputation

SLC product

Between 1993 and 2002, leaders from environmental groups, forest companies, First Nations and local communities on the province of British Columbia (BC)'s West Coast came together to learn and innovate their way out of a protracted and complex conflict over logging practices. The knowledge and relationships built in this small region have led to the creation of new societal institutions and ongoing intersectoral collaborations in the Central and North Coast of the province.

Description

The West Coast of Canada is punctured by forested deep mountainous fjords and inlets that are inhabited by scattered communities of foresters and First Nations people. Clayoquot Sound faces the open Pacific with a large sandy spit. At one end of the spit is a community of loggers and at the other a community dependent on tourism. Each represents an important part of the provincial economy.

Government-led consultation fails (1980–93)

As the dispute over logging flared in the late 1980s, the provincial government of BC set up a series of task forces and committees to develop a land use plan that would be acceptable to all parties. None succeeded. Environmentalists walked away from the table, saying they were tired of a policy of 'talk and log'.

Finally, in April 1993, the government stepped in to resolve the matter by issuing a new set of policies, called the Clayoquot Land Use Decision. The new policy would protect one-third of the Sound from logging. The rest of the land could be logged, but operations would be subject to new rules requiring industry to consider wildlife, recreational and scenic values.

All sides were unhappy with the land use decision. The forest company MacMillan Bloedel (MB) felt its rights to log had been constrained, unions complained about the loss of jobs, environmentalists were dissatisfied with the amount of land protected and the First Nations felt they had been excluded from decisions affecting their traditional territory. Linda Coady,[1] then VP of Environment for MB, described it as a 'zero sum game . . . in which the only acceptable outcome is for one side to win at the expense of the other' (Coady 1999).

Blockades, civil disobedience and boycott (1993–97)

In the summer of 1993, the battle escalated. Environmental groups organised a Clayoquot Sound Peace Camp, which attracted protesters from throughout North America and Europe. At least 9,000 people participated in demonstrations against clear-cut logging. More than 800 people were arrested in the largest act of civil disobedience in Canadian history when protesters massed to block logging roads and climbed trees to protect them from cutting. Suddenly, Clayoquot Sound was in the headlines around the world.

In October 1993, the government responded by initiating the Scientific Panel for Sustainable Forest Practices in Clayoquot Sound, an independent panel of First Nations and scientific experts. The Panel's mandate was to develop world-class standards for sustainable forest management by combining traditional and scientific knowledge. Two years later, the Panel's report recommended that clear-cutting be replaced by variable retention forestry, an approach that would leave some trees standing in each area, to protect the health of the forest ecosystem.

The parties remained unhappy. In 1997, Greenpeace launched a consumer boycott of BC's forest products in Europe and the United States, promoting their cause with demonstrations and direct mail. As a result of the campaign, three major British home supply chains agreed to stop buying from companies engaging in clear-cut logging in BC. In the US, Xerox, 3M, FedEx and several other companies followed suit. The boycott deeply concerned MB's board of directors.

That summer, the environmental movement returned to Clayoquot Sound with another round of demonstrations on King Island, where logging had begun. Greenpeace ships sailed into Vancouver harbour. Timber workers, angered by the protests, surrounded the ships with a chain of logs, preventing their movement. The

---

1   In November 2002 Linda became Vice-President of WWF, Pacific Region.

workers' union sued Greenpeace, demanding compensation for wages lost because of the protests.

Clayoquot First Nations create opportunities for a new conversation (1996–98)

At the same time that the Panel was developing its recommendations, the provincial government was negotiating with the First Nations to resolve their aboriginal land claims. The Canadian courts supported the claims and the First Nations people engaged in blockades and other civil disobedience to get action to settle them.

Between 1996 and 1998, First Nations leaders from Clayoquot Sound convened a series of meetings between MB managers and the environmental group leaders. Some of the meetings also included loggers and community representatives. A few of the meetings were held around the fire in longhouses in remote First Nations communities.

'With a modern-day Treaty process having begun in earnest in BC, the aboriginal peoples of Clayoquot Sound found themselves with the moral authority to cast the swing vote in the whole controversy,' recalls Linda.

> They had the effective political power to either discredit Greenpeace's international market campaign or blow MB's defences to smithereens. What this led to was a journey in which both MB and the environmental groups were like two convicts escaped from the chain gang manacled together. Like it or not, [we] had to work out a solution both could live with.

With the interventions by the First Nations, the dynamics of the conversation between the company and environmental groups changed. Both the company representatives and environmental group leaders were forced to communicate directly with each other and to listen to understand rather than defend.

New joint venture company and forest project

In late 1997, MB announced its intention to establish a new commercial joint venture sustainable logging company. It was called Iisaak (meaning 'respect' in the Nuu-Chah-Nulth language) Forest Resources. MB transferred a portion of its logging rights in Clayoquot Sound to Iisaak, which was 49% owned by MB and 51% by the Nuu-Chah-Nulth First Nations. Iisaak was committed to traditional aboriginal values and respect for the environment. It promised to practise variable retention logging and to seek third-party certification of its timber, with the intention of seeking markets for its premium-priced products among environmentally aware customers.

In late 1997, MB's board appointed a new CEO, Tom Stephens. He was convinced that MB needed to change the way it operated in order to regain its 'social licence to operate' in BC. In a highly unusual move, Stephens invited leaders of the most critical environmental groups to his home to discuss their concerns about clear-cutting. During the meeting, Stephens announced his intention to launch The

Forest Project, a $1 million project to develop an economically feasible plan to end clear-cutting.

In June 1998, MB publicly announced it was phasing out clear-cutting in favour of variable retention logging on all of its private and public timberlands in BC, thus becoming the first company to break what some environmentalists called the 'clear-cutting cartel'.

After a period of intense dialogue, an agreement was signed with four of the five most vocal and critical environmental organisations. The environmentalists agreed to call off all blockades and boycotts directed at MB in exchange for the company's commitment to sustainable harvesting, respect for aboriginal values and an acknowledgement of the value of eco-tourism. This was a pivotal and highly unusual turn of events.

Conflict shifted to the Central and North Coast (1998–2000)

In 1998, conflict shifted from Clayoquot to the Central and North Coast of BC. A larger coalition of environmental groups launched the 'Great Bear Rainforest' campaign to promote the preservation of forests on the coast. The campaign targeted a number of companies operating in the region, but not MB.

During this period, the environmental groups and companies faced considerable pressure from First Nations, government, international purchasers of wood products and local communities to resolve their differences. In August 1999, lumber retailer Home Depot announced it would phase out products made from 'endangered forests'. German pulp and publishing companies also threatened to cancel contracts with the forest companies.

Ceasefire and forming new organisations

Following months of dialogue and negotiation, the companies and environmental NGOs (ENGOs) agreed to a 'ceasefire' in April 2000. They agreed to a 'conflict-free' period to allow planning processes to proceed. It was 'a safe place to go to think, to talk, to air things,' said one participant. 'As companies,' adds Linda,

> we had to create a safe place where we could go to examine alternatives
> to the status quo. Getting the licence to do this within our own organi-
> sations was hard enough, let alone doing so with groups with whom we
> were in a highly adversarial conflict.

A new multi-stakeholder group called the Joint Solutions Project (JSP) was created in August 2000 to act as a catalyst for change in the region. JSP members included many of the same environmental group leaders who had been active in Clayoquot Sound, but also had participation from a broader cross-section of forest companies.

Another change agent, the Turning Point Initiative, was established to address environmental and economic issues of importance to First Nations and to ensure that government and other parties were mindful of the rights and interests of First Nations.

Individuals and groups withdrew from the process and rejoined at various points along the way. The industry and environmental caucuses struggled to clarify their own agendas before they could participate in the JSP. First Nations groups on the coast struggled to agree on their common agenda before joining with the David Suzuki Foundation to form Turning Point.

Loggers, government agencies and local communities also had to make their voices and interests heard in what was initially a dialogue mainly between environmental groups and companies.

Innovative agreement for the coast (2001)

Over the next 18 months the JSP and Turning Point met a number of times to discuss new ideas around ecosystem planning, impact mitigation, community economic development and aboriginal rights. Both foundations and the government provided financial support. The dialogue was intense and focused on learning and innovation. 'This exercise is really about collaborative inquiry and learning,' comments Linda.

> It is not about stakeholder negotiations on social licence issues, but the next-generation model where we ask, 'How do we learn together? How do we innovate together despite the fact that occasionally we hate each other and we can't get along?'

During this process, stakeholder leaders also had to maintain the fragile support of their organisations. The backlash from industry and the environmental groups was strong. Company representatives were criticised inside their own organisations for 'selling out' to the environmentalists.

After a long and often contentious process, the groups jointly developed a plan for moving forward. On 4 April 2001 a landmark agreement on land use on the Central Coast was announced by the government of BC, along with a new protocol between coastal First Nations and the Province on interim measures and planning.

SLC features

Communities acting as intersectoral actors

The First Nations, Uculet and Tofino communities all have government powers but they also act as civil society organisations. They are close-knit groups that are fighting for closely held and distinctive values.

Learning new ways to learn

The Forest Project 'was essentially an exercise in adaptive management and organisational learning,' reflects Linda. 'The most significant result is not so much the particular changes we came up with. Rather it is the fact we learned some new ways to learn.'

Building a new shared goal

> At some point, *commented Linda Coady*, we all began to put more time and energy into achieving a shared goal. The shared outcome didn't belong to either side when the dispute began. Nor would it likely have ever been foreseen as a viable option by either side when the dispute began. So it wasn't really a product of consensus or compromise. Instead, it was an outcome of continual interaction and constant redefinition of the situation and the options for dealing with it.

Transferring societal learning

The relationships and learning from Clayoquot provided the basis for building a strategy for the entire coast of BC. This was quite easy since the parties were so closely related in both locations. It provided a bonus return on the investment in Clayoquot.

Creating safe places

The major groups—business, government, community-based organisations—created their independent forums to meet and identify their positions. As the interactions between the groups matured, they also created places and periods of time where they met collaboratively to investigate and develop innovative approaches.

Producing losers

SLC changes are not simple win–win ones. Many of the forestry workers viewed themselves as losers in the story. Although the government provided transition assistance, good union jobs were lost and the low-paying new tourism jobs were poor substitutes. Others said the jobs would have disappeared eventually in any case, once the clear-cutting was complete.

Reference

Coady, L. (1999) 'Good Stuff You Likely Won't Find on Anybody's Website: Reflections of a Corporate Environmental Manager in the 1990s BC Coastal Forest Industry' (Doug Little Memorial Lecture; University of Northern British Columbia, Prince George, BC Canada).

Case name

Centre for Technology Development and economic development in India

Author

Steve Waddell

Case type

Community-focused SLC

Location

Bangalore region, India

Sectoral context

India has a strong national government tradition, with the state being seen as the major engine of development. The 1990s were characterised by moves to decentralise and deregulate to a modest degree. The business sector is sophisticated in some industries—Bangalore, for example, is well-known for its computer technology—and weak in others such as banking and finance which has been government-dominated. Civil society is quite robust, with relatively strong labour unions and many non-governmental organisations involved in various development aspects. Academic institutions play an important role and are largely government-funded.

Major participants (agriculture and food processing)

- Hindustan Lever
- Horticultural Producers' Co-operative Marketing and Processing Society
- United States Agency for International Development
- Government of the State of Karnataka
- Indian Institute of Sciences
- Association of Women Entrepreneurs of Karnataka

Societal goal

- Encourage, develop and globally commercialise indigenous technologies

Civil society goal

- Upliftment of the people

Government goal

- Economic and technological development
- Application of knowledge developed by universities

Business goal

- Development of targeted industries
- Influence public policy
- Meet social responsibility obligations

SLC product

The Centre for Technology Development (CTD) initiative has created a system that applies knowledge developed in post-secondary institutions to produce new enterprises that spread benefits to a broad cross-section of society. In agriculture and food production the focus has been on small farmers and producers, and connecting them to large businesses and the formal market. This has included developing greenhouses and mist chambers, a potato industry, new crop introduction programmes, vermiculture, fruit and vegetable packing facility, business incubator, quality control and product development laboratories and a food technology database. This is done through unusual intersectoral organising.

Description

On the sprawling central plains of the state of Karnataka in southern India an economic development initiative called the Centre for Technology Development (CTD) makes interesting partners of an array of organisations. This includes organisations involved in informatics, dry land agriculture, new metals production, venture capital and food processing. The members of this unusual array have three things in common: they all build on knowledge resources, social capital and a particularly rich local economic development potential.

CTD was founded in 1989 with support of the United States Agency for International Development (USAID; an agency of the American government). CTD's mission is to 'encourage and develop indigenous technologies and help commercialise them globally'. It frames technology as the 'main propulsive input' in its development work, and aims to build linkages between academic institutions and those who can benefit from the application of the institutions' knowledge, such as small farmers, entrepreneurs and manufacturers. This is seen as:

[A] paradigm shift from the older elements of cheap land, cheap labour, low-cost financial assistance and low taxes to interrelated industries with access to technology, highly trained technical workers, venture capital type of financial assistance, high value addition in the production of market-driven goods and services that are globally competitive (CTD 1995).

CTD is the result of a paradox noted by USAID. In the mid-1980s India spent approximately 1% of GNP on research and development and had the fifth largest pool of technical personnel in the world. However, it was experiencing slow growth and had yet to reap significant commercial benefits from its R&D investment. USAID concluded that a major reason for this was the weak link between the basic research and industry needs.

USAID created a $10 million bilateral project in 1989 for a regional development initiative in the Indian State of Karnataka, which became CTD. USAID assistance to CTD also included technical assistance, human resources development, state-of-the-art equipment to upgrade the existing institutions, and facilitating venture capital finance to small and medium companies from venture capital/financial institutions. Three government agencies contributed about $150,000 each to an endowment and a board of 12 leading business, government and academic individuals was established.

CTD was designed as a ten-year project that would build on local strengths by developing four self-sustaining operations—food processing, informatics, new materials and dry-land agriculture. Each of these became a separate non-profit called an Applied Technology Centre with its own board. To simply convey the essence of CTD and its societal learning and change role, this case focuses on the food processing and agriculture operations.

CTD provides (1) new project proposal review, (2) contract relationships, (3) financial accounting and (4) evaluation and monitoring. The critical factor that makes CTD work is the participation of senior people with both substantial expertise and social capital networks. There are three categories of individuals: full-time employees (only two at CTD itself), senior retired people who often work 20 hours a week or more on a pro bono basis, and a broader support network that includes people on the boards. The first two categories form the 'working group'.

The 'retired but not tired' group of pro bono workers is particularly critical. In India retirement comes early, at age 57 for government employees. CTD and its associated NGOs have engaged very senior retirees, including chief secretaries of the State of Karnataka, a former vice-chairman of a community college, and a former bank CEO. These are people who are both intimately familiar with the way things work, and have personal relationships that help them get things done and obtain information necessary to successfully develop projects.

CTD is described in its *Administration Manual* as a 'virtual organisation'. Its office is described as a 'clubhouse or minimalist office only for essential meetings'. The Secretariat is physically located in a very informal office on the campus of the Indian Institute of Sciences (IISc) in Bangalore. There are no individual offices, but rather a large space where the regular employees have their own desks and the others work informally around a large table. Informal exchanges are common as individuals develop their own particular initiatives and do their work. This means that the cost of CTD administration is minimal, since the office space is donated by IISc and senior workers provide pro bono service. In fact, the endowment provides sufficient cash flow from investments to cover staff costs.

CTD plays an important network-building function. It sponsors conferences to share information and bring people together. It organises people into groups. For example, it took a leading role in organising the venture capital industry in India, and in Bangalore it stimulated a Buyer Seller Development Initiative to connect major industries to small and medium-sized enterprises.

This connecting role is also a critical function of the affiliated CTD-created NGOs. Agri-Tech focuses on connecting new agriculture technology to small farmers. In partnership with the University of Agricultural Sciences and a private business called Indo-American Hybrids, Agri-Tech has developed a technology called poly-houses. This is a very-low-cost greenhouse which is affordable for small farmers. Agri-Tech has undertaken demonstration projects and through the government organised subsidies for initial users of the technology to help spread its use. The farmers participating in these programmes are identified in part through the network of rural banks that can identify early adopters of new approaches who are influential. The state's agriculture ministry is engaged in training farmers in use of the technology.

These types of initiatives are creating long-term sustainability for the NGOs through their commercial agreements such as with the polyhouses. Another example is a new company established in partnership with a private firm called Sterling Tree Magnum Ltd and the University of Agricultural Sciences, which is commercialising a new approach to potato reproduction. Seed potatoes that are traditionally used for reproduction do not fare well in the warm climate of Karnataka. The new approach develops seed from potato flowers.

Development of these projects moves through five stages. In the first there are discussions to identify mutual interests among the various partners and opinions about potential impact. In the second a specific project is defined and draft scopes of work are exchanged to create a proposal. Then the proposal is taken to CTD for review, and if necessary to find financing. The fourth stage is actual project development, secured by a memorandum of understanding which defines each party's role and responsibilities. If these stages are successful, the fifth stage involves commercialisation of the production and application of the jointly developed technology.

Agri-Tech's board and pro bono staff also have high social capital, far beyond what an organisation of this size would generally warrant. It includes a senior staff member from the Indian Forest Service, the Chief Engineer of the Karnataka Electricity Board and the former head of the National Dairy Research Institute. 'We're professionals in project execution,' emphasises Board member Mr P.R. Rao.

Agri-Tech is connected to another CTD NGO called the Centre for Food Processing (CFP) through CTD, a common board member, pro bono workers and the food production chain. When established in the early 1990s, only 1% of food consumption in India comprised processed food. Urbanisation and export markets suggested this was a good industry to develop, and CFP was established with the mission 'to work to the development of a strong and modern food processing industry in India' (CFP 1996).

'The idea is to sensitise people to the possibilities, and get people into producing them,' says CFP director Mr G. Asvanthanarayan. This emphasises the incubation stage of development of the industry and the need to strategically influence production. These goals have led to establishing consultancy services, a food technology database, common service facilities with other organisations, education programmes and facilitating interaction of diverse parties.

Consultancy is seen as the most important service. It is distinguished by an 'activist approach', reflecting an altruistic culture aiming for betterment of people. This has led to a focus on small and medium farmers and producers—a market overlooked by more traditional consultants because of its lack of sophistication, market orientation, capacity for fees, and scale production. Moreover, women are the traditional small processed food processors and they lack access to education and credit.

CFP has created a new network of services, including an analytical quality control laboratory, a product development laboratory, a business incubator and a produce sorting facility. Some of these are brand-new CFP creations and some are upgrades of historic facilities. All are distinguished by their new comprehensive network structure and partnership development approach. The laboratories are co-developed with the research institutes and the packing facility with the Horticultural Producers' Co-operative Marketing and Processing Society (HOPCOMS).

HOPCOMS is a 9,500-member farmers' co-operative. It received a capital investment through CTD. 'In the Indian context, the result is entirely new,' says G. Asvanthanarayan. 'Traditionally our fruit comes to a wholesaler who's not interested in grading because it's too much work.' Grading reduces waste (25% discard is not uncommon) by encouraging farmers to bring fruit that is ripe and in good condition. Working with HOPCOMS, CFP has introduced simple plastic stackable crates to hold produce that was previously crushed by stacking in big piles.

A business incubator for processed food producers has been constructed with a 400-member women's small business association called the Association of Women Entrepreneurs of Karnataka (AWAKE). Another has been developed at a girls' high school with the support of private companies Hawkins and Unilever's Lipton Masterline.

CFP's board is similarly a social capital powerhouse with three categories: generalists, food scientists and finance/industry representatives. The food company Hindustan Lever is on the board and contributed to an endowment with the rationale that it will benefit from strengthening of the food industry.

SLC features

Creating social capital

Although CTD emphasises technology drawn from Bangalore's research institutes as the core ingredient in its success, the key work of CTD is to create linkages between organisations to make their individual efforts more effective. The strategy of CTD is to use and build social capital (personal relationships and organisation structures) to apply human capital (specialised knowledge and technology).

Leveraging resources

The CTD approach is very low-cost. It leverages resources from participating organisations, such as the free office from IISc. It leverages professional resources by aspiring to the altruistic goal of 'upliftment of the people' to procure pro bono work.

Connecting across social class

A classic challenge for economic development initiatives is to distribute the benefits to marginalised people. Those who have power typically access the benefits much more easily. This is particularly true of foreign aid interventions, where agencies are easily manipulated by their lack of local knowledge and dependence on government relationships. CTD engages people from the economic and political elites and connects them to small farmers and co-operatives.

Creating flexibility to overcome rigidity

The 'retired but not tired' are having a lot of fun working in CTD. In their former senior positions their entrepreneurial spirit and insight about what *could be* was often blocked by the rules and responsibilities that came with their jobs. A major problem with India's traditional state-centred development strategy was rigidity that comes with bureaucracy. CTD creates flexible centres of activity with people who are well connected to the state system, and through their new positions can help make its programmes more effective.

Focusing on useful work

'CTD is something you do, not a place you go to,' commented CTD director Mr P.C. Nyak. It deliberately focuses on valued work, rather than accoutrements of status and prestige such as offices and perquisites. Moreover, it begins by coolly analysing a situation, the opportunities and problems. Rather than accepting traditional barriers and reasons why something cannot be done, it works around them to find innovative solutions.

Designing full systems stewardship

Development is often hampered because parts within a supply chain are non-existent or dysfunctional. Particular businesses may be successful, but their own development is hampered because the whole chain is not developed. This is a classic tragedy of the production commons, since there is no one responsible for the whole chain. Agri-Tech and CFP are doing the system organising as stewards for the whole chain. (See also the Philippine rice example, page 62.)

Leading with the common good

CTD has managed to combine both altruism and more tangible benefits to engage a broad range of people and organisations. Everyone can feel good about the altruistic goals. But, in fact, business understands it is getting valued benefit from the building of industry infrastructure, and government is getting valued benefit by increasing the impact of its programmes and research institutes.

References

CFP (Centre for Food Processing) (1996 approx.) 'Organization Profile' (Bangalore, India: CFP).

CTD (Centre for Technology Development) (1995 approx.) 'Centre for Technology Development' (flyer; Bangalore, India: CTD4).

Case name
The Global Reporting Initiative and corporate transformation

Author
Steve Waddell

Case type

Global change

Location

Global; secretariat: Amsterdam, The Netherlands

Sectoral context

The global arena following World War II was dominated by agreements between governments and inter-governmental organisations such as the United Nations and World Bank. However, the ability of governments to take effective global action is weak. Business is the strongest global actor with large global operating structures. Its role has grown significantly since the late 1980s when the Soviet Union collapsed and governments started promoting international business as agents of development. Civil society is comparatively weak globally, in large part due to the fact that much of its strength arises from close relationships to communities which means building close relationships globally is problematic.

Major participants

- Businesses including many of the world's largest corporations
- Non-governmental organisations including many leading activist bodies
- Labour union federations
- Intermediating groups such as research organisations and professional associations

Societal goal

- Change norms, rules and organisations' activity to achieve sustainable development

Civil society goal

- Make businesses accountable for their social, economic and environmental impacts

Government goal

- Government is not a direct participant, but is an indirect supporter with the goal of creating a voluntary process for business–civil society relationships and sustainability of business activity

Business goal

- Create a global reporting standard for businesses' social, economic and environmental impacts
- Proactively address public relations and risk issues that can arise from corporate operations

SLC product

Most approaches to reporting on organisations' social, economic and environmental performance are driven by defensive legal compliance and public relations imperatives. Traditionally, reporting systems are the responsibility of one organisational sector (government in the case of mandatory reporting, business in the case of most voluntary reporting). While improvements in performance are an espoused goal, in fact the systems are quite static and generate only modest experimentation. Moreover, they do not address the fundamental need to somehow raise standards (change the rules of the game) in a coherent way for all organisations. In an era of globalisation and easy geographic movement for many businesses, the ability for national governments to do this has become severely circumscribed.

The Global Reporting Initiative (GRI) is a bold new approach that aims to overcome these limitations by creating globally multi-stakeholder processes and a culture of learning and intense experimentation. The civil society and business participants build mutual accountability. The diversity of their goals while working together is creating a dynamic force and progress on difficult issues such as HIV/AIDS and vehicle emission standards. The broad and open participatory approach supports the wide dissemination of new knowledge.

Description

For three dreary, rainy days in November 2000 an odd collection of people met in a large theatre on the campus of George Washington University in Washington, DC. They included about 400 activists, academics, business people and government and inter-governmental officials from around the world. They were drawn by common concerns about sustainability and ways to meld their diverse viewpoints and interests into a new global sustainability reporting framework. The meeting was the Second International Symposium of the Global Reporting Initiative.

Allen White, Transition Director for GRI, explained to the assembled people that GRI was a response to a reporting problem and the need for reporting was well recognised. White was also director of the business and sustainability group of Tellus Institute. His position, academic manner and environmental research activist credentials made him a credible figure for the diverse symposium participants. 'Managers, investors, and citizens receive diverse, incompatible, incomplete information from companies,' said White. 'Companies face diverse, incompatible, and increasingly voluminous information requests from internal managers, investors, NGOs, citizens, and government.' GRI could create coherency out of a muddle.

Midway through the conference, NGOs announced that they were holding a special meeting for NGOs only. They had doubts about what they heard. Who was in control? It felt like a top-down process. Who was really going to benefit from this work? Was GRI really serious about engaging NGOs? Would voluntary standards really be useful?

While it was still too early to declare the GRI a complete success four years later, its record in pulling together discordant voices and the widespread support it has received are impressive. The United Nation's Global Compact is promoting it as an international standard. Alison Maitland of the *Financial Times* commented in December 2002 that 'One particular (reporting) framework—the GRI—is emerging as a potential leader because of its broad foundations and international reach.' Organisations and people as diverse as Greenpeace, British Prime Minister Tony Blair and corporate CEOs have spoken in support of the GRI. By 2004 GRI had documented hundreds of organisations—many of them global corporations such as 3M, AT&T, BHP Billiton and British Airways—in 24 countries, that had applied the GRI framework.

The GRI idea began with the Boston-based Coalition for Environmentally Responsible Economies (CERES)—a coalition of environmental NGOs and shareholder activists that advocates to corporations that they endorse a set of environmental principles.[1] In the second half of the 1990s CERES began a dialogue with its signatory corporations which included General Motors, Sunoco and other *Fortune* 500 companies. CERES executive director Bob Massie, also Chair of the GRI Steering Committee which nurtured GRI into existence, recalls that 'There was consensus that common global disclosure standards were needed . . . people with different interests and motivation all wanted the same thing for different reasons.'

By the time of the dialogue, sustainability management and reporting had exploded into a wide variety of approaches. ISO 14000 was an international business-led model imitating the successful ISO 9000 quality management standards; the SA8000 was an international civil society initiative by the Council on Economic Priorities in New York; CERES promoted environmental principles and reporting to American business; the Caux Roundtable produced a code of conduct for businesses; the MacBride Principles guided investment in Northern Ireland; in the United Kingdom the Institute for Social and Ethical Accountability produced a stakeholder framework called AA1000: governments, with Danes and Dutch in the lead, were producing their own reporting frameworks. From nothing in 1990, a

---

1   When GRI began, CERES focused on environmental principles. It now includes broader sustainability principles.

decade later there were over 2,200 corporate environmental and sustainability reports (White 2000).

A study of environmental reporting systems, *Green Metrics*, drafted in 1997, provided an overview of the field and revealed that there was already a substantial amount of common ground on which to build. A strategy to unify rather than replace the numerous other reporting initiatives was adopted in recognition of the valuable work of others and the amount of commitment of key stakeholders to the work. GRI's vision became: 'To support global progress towards sustainable development, the GRI Sustainability Reporting Guidelines will become the generally accepted, broadly adopted worldwide framework for preparing, communicating and requesting information about corporate performance.'

The NGO coalition structure of CERES and the nature of its relationship with big business made a multi-stakeholder approach for GRI a natural choice. Measurement specialists were attracted to the prospect of an effective common framework, the NGOs were inspired by the broader vision of what this could mean for sustainability, and business people were quite keen on the creation of a unifying system that adequately reflected their needs and concerns.

In order to reduce the competitive reflex, Massie invited other organisations to participate in a two-year experiment to see whether there was a basis for establishing a common disclosure guideline. To alleviate their suspicions, Massie promised that everyone who wanted to participate would be given a role; that everyone who was interested would be kept informed; that CERES would bear the bulk of the direct costs; that decisions would be reached openly and by consensus; and that, if the GRI turned out to be a success, CERES would spin it off into an independent organisation with a new board of directors. 'We saw ourselves as stewards of a process,' says Massie.

The founders did not see GRI as a sustainability advocacy group. Rather, it focuses on the challenge of harmonisation, disclosure and information issues to make sustainable accounting a reality. In contrast to other approaches dominated and owned either by advocacy organisations or business groups, GRI is a multi-stakeholder tool for people to realise sustainability. Application of GRI guidelines is voluntary, in order to create an experimental, learning and participative approach. The presence of NGOs is critical to creating legitimacy and generating the momentum and change that business or government voluntary schemes lack.

Government agencies were not invited to participate, to avoid any misconceptions about the voluntary nature of GRI's reporting system. However, by early 1998 CERES and the United Nations Environment Programme (UNEP) developed a partnership. UNEP does not have enforcement powers that might confuse GRI's voluntary nature. It provided a degree of legitimacy internationally and an international network that were valued. In addition, UNEP committed $3 million, which provided critical financial support in addition to the initial funding by foundations.

Originally, GRI focused on environmental concerns. In early 1998 the multi-stakeholder GRI Steering Committee decided to broaden the original focus beyond environmental concerns and to consider sustainability more broadly. This meant that interest in GRI broadened, and GRI gained in value and distinctiveness because fewer reporting approaches focused on this broad range of sustainability indicators.

From 1997 to 2002 when a permanent independent institution was established, GRI described its work in terms of three basic tasks:

1. Creating the reporting framework (*Guidelines*)

2. Developing a multi-stakeholder process (MSP)

3. Creating a permanent institution

To identify a permanent location GRI publicised its needs to national governments. The Dutch government responded with the most generous offer of support, and in 2002 when GRI became an independent institution it moved to Amsterdam. By the end of that year, Ernst Ligteringen, formerly with Oxfam International, was appointed GRI executive director.

SLC features

Acting as a steward

During its development, CERES was positioned as a 'steward' for the interests of multiple stakeholders who had not yet organised themselves sufficiently to respond to the GRI challenge. This contrasts with most other reporting approaches where organisations develop an approach that they own as an individual organisation or as a restricted group of organisations.

Unifying diverse approaches

Rather than emphasising its uniqueness in competition with other reporting approaches, GRI developed a strategy to embrace other approaches and bring their leaders into its fold.

Integrating science and subjectivity

It is common to approach controversial issues by aiming to establish a set of agreed-on scientific facts. However, this process is usually separated from the politics of non-scientific views. For example, with climate change the International Panel on Climate Change was a scientific body separate from the body negotiating the Kyoto Protocol. In GRI the diverse viewpoints mixed politics and science much more closely from the start.

Emphasising multi-stakeholder processes

The MSP quality of GRI activities was reflected in all its activities. Business, government, environmentalists, technical experts and academics were integrated into its numerous working groups to develop the *Guidelines*. Working groups were given very specific terms of reference and were immediately disbanded when they had completed their work.

Pacing and planning development

Quite early on, the GRI founders established a five-year development framework to create an independent organisation. It was unusually well planned.

Recognising intermediating organisations

GRI has created a membership category of 'intermediating organisations'. These include research organisations and professional associations. This is an innovation particularly unique to GRI, and recognises that some organisations act as bridges between sectors.

Integrating learning

Development of the GRI was characterised by a primary 'learning' quality. The whole initiative was permeated with recognition that something very complex was being attempted, there were few clear rules and a spirit of experimentation was important to achieve the goals. This applied to its organisational development and development of the reporting framework. When major questions arose, typically, diverse views and expertise were sought and a synthesis or innovation was created appropriate for GRI.

Reference

White, A. (2000) Address to the Second International Symposium of the GRI, Washington, DC.

Case name
Madagascar road-building

Author

Steve Waddell

Case type

Infrastructure-based SLC

Location

Madagascar

Sectoral context

All three sectors in Madagascar are weak and must be considered in the context of a peasant culture characterised by pre-industrial social relationships. About 80% of the population depends on agriculture with small land-holdings and dispersed villages.

Major participants

- United States Agency for International Development (USAID)
- Chemonics International
- Private road-builders
- Government of Madagascar
- Road users' associations (Associations Usagers de Pistes; AUPs)
- Capacity-building NGOs

Societal goal

- Create a sustainable strategy for rural road-building and maintenance

Civil society goal

- Enhance security
- Connect parishes and communities

Government goal

- Address its responsibility to ensure provision and maintenance of rural roads
- Address constraints in agricultural growth

Business goal

- Create a new profitable business by working with road users to train them to build and maintain roads
- Improve access to markets

SLC product

Usually road-building and maintenance are seen as something done directly by government or contracted to private companies. In Madagascar the government demonstrated its incapacity to do the work as rural roads under its responsibility fell into serious disrepair. The government did not have the financial resources to contract out the work to private companies and the population is far too poor to afford toll roads maintained by private companies.

An alternative approach based on traditional practice and organised into a modern and reliable system was developed by creating road users' associations. The approach echoes those seen earlier in developed countries, but with a 21st-century framework. The mass-membership civil society organisations set tolls, negotiate with government for subsidies and organise building and maintenance. In contrast to the government and private alternatives, this approach produces a high level of accountability and provision of roads based on local needs.

Description

Madagascar is among the poorest countries in the world economically with 70% of the population in poverty. Per capita income through most of the 1990s declined, in part due to a high birth rate. Adult literacy is about 80%. There is a severe loss of forest cover in a country renowned for its unique ecological treasures. This results in severe problems of erosion.

In the early 1990s the road system reflected this general state of decay. Fewer than 5,500 km were paved and about 245,000 km are little more than earth tracks that bad weather can make impassable for three to six months a year. Overlapping government jurisdictions, financial problems and a lack of technical resources conspire with the difficult terrain and weather to make road-building a formidable challenge. 'Building roads in Madagascar is like putting a man on the moon,' commented USAID officer Dale Rachmeler.

The town of Fianar in the south central highlands of Madagascar is a provincial capital and a regional agricultural centre. The cyclone of 1986 wiped out the bridge most directly linking Fianar to the commune of Kalalao. The event had significant repercussions. Anyone travelling from the village over the dirt roads to the provincial capital would need four hours to cover 23 km on a circuitous route. Kalalao resident Philibert said it not only made getting produce to market difficult. 'It was a problem of security,' he explained as he pointed a rifle out of the second-storey window of his farmhouse to demonstrate how he had to protect his crops, livestock and family from bandits. Police could not get to the village and the region devolved into lawlessness.

The road problem was complicated by confusing governmental jurisdictions. The commune of Kalalao contained only 13 km of the total roadway between the village and the paved national highway. A second commune contained 9 km and another 12 km. These communes were also in two provincial *sous-préfectures*.

A priest was instrumental in the formation of committees in the communes to address the road problem. The government said there was no money for repairs. A request for help was sent to Chemonics International, a contractor leading a USAID programme. A feasibility study asked three questions. One concerned the traditional engineering issues and costs. A second analysed the financial impact of the road and potential traffic, which revealed substantial agricultural potential. The third question dealt with the way villagers interacted and their potential for working together to help both build and maintain the road—the presence of the commune committees provided positive indicators.

Recommendations by Chemonics to proceed were approved first by a joint commune–national government committee and then by a USAID–Chemonics–national government committee. The project proceeded with Chemonics undertaking to support the communes to organise themselves to take responsibility for the roads in their jurisdictions.

In January 1997 social organisers employed by Chemonics began working with all the communities along the road linking Kalalao to the national highway. Five of 12 *quartiers* making up Kalalao commune had particular interest in the roads and identified delegates for a communal road committee.

- National
- Provincial
- Sous-préfecture
- Commune
- Quartier

Box 3.1 Levels of Madagascar government

Over the next year three activities ensued. One concerned the levels of government and the responsibility for roads. In mid-1997 the provincial government officially passed authority over its section of the road to the communal governments in a ceremony known as *transfer de gérance*. The authority was summarised in three points: (1) administration of the road which includes the ability to levy tolls, (2) protection of people travelling on the roads and (3) maintenance of the roads.

The second activity was the rehabilitation of the roads themselves. Even before the social organisers were working in Kalalao, Chemonics was organising the actual road reconstruction. It defined the work to be done and put out the contract for bid by private, for-profit contractors. The bids stipulated that the villagers were to be hired for the road-building as much as possible and taught the skills necessary for road maintenance. The companies had to agree to work with villagers to define where the roads were to be placed to ensure that the roads are in line with local needs, history and beliefs.

A third activity was the formation of official AUPs (road users' associations), with the help of the social organisers. They began with provisional committees, and over about half a year the committees became formal with a defined structure, papers of incorporation and officers trained in the rudiments of budgets and running of a non-governmental organisation. Defining a maintenance budget, estimating the expenses and identifying income were major issues. The budget provides for income for road maintenance from AUP membership fees, contributions by the local governments and tolls. After a year of operating experience, a second ceremony, the *transfer de compétence*, formally moved authority for the road from the commune to the AUPs.

Kalalao has a mass-membership organisation with the goal of all adult residents of the *quartiers* being members and paying a fee of about US$0.10. The *quartiers* embrace 1,500 people. Each elects delegates to be communication links between the residents and the AUPs; they are also responsible for collecting membership fees. Within six months of defining the fee in Kalalao, 75% had paid. Those who do not pay may have their resident certificates—necessary to access government services such as schools—withheld by the commune.

The AUPs have three general membership meetings a year, where tolls and other issues are discussed and a budget approved. The idea of tolls for financing arose only after discussion of alternatives and the lack of government funding. Paying the tolls has led the users to be particularly vigilant when road repairs are needed and to keep in touch with their AUP delegates.

To depoliticise the process of approving road-building contracts and reduce opportunities for corruption, the responses to the request for bids were reviewed by a national committee of Chemonics and government ministry representatives, which made recommendations to another committee of government representatives and USAID. Both large international construction companies and small local ones won contracts; after trying both, Chemonics concluded that the local ones are generally better because they work better with the local people and are cheaper—even though they do not have access to the same quality road-building equipment and require more supervision. In Kalalao the work of construction provided an important source of income for about 40 villagers, including many women, over a four-month period. The project was completed by mid-1997.

The impact of the roads was felt immediately. Philibert believes their improvement is directly tied to the end of banditry in the region. Now that they can actually get their produce to markets, villagers are adapting intensive agricultural techniques that have increased their production elevenfold in comparison to traditional output. Philibert estimates that his 12 hectares of land produce 65 tonnes, of which only 5 tonnes is retained for local use.

SLC features

Formalising of sectoral realignment

The major government innovation is represented by the *transfers de compétence* and *gérance*. These represent a formal way to change the roles of the sectors with respect to rural road-building and maintenance.

Companies redefining their work

The road-building companies have had to redefine their work from building roads to building villagers' capacity to build roads.

Building on local capacity

As much work as possible is done by local villagers. Moreover, experience demonstrated that local contractors are better than international ones because of their local knowledge.

Finding new resources

The government did not have sufficient resources to provide road maintenance through the traditional system. By organising villagers to take care of their roads themselves and introducing tolls, costs are reduced and new revenues raised.

Reducing corruption

The traditional approach to road-building was rife with corruption, as road-building companies paid politicians and bureaucrats to be selected for work. The new and transparent process of bidding with a national government and Chemonics committee has addressed this issue. In the longer term, as contracts will be negotiated and managed by AUPs with contracts approved at users' meetings, corruption should continue to be managed.

Enhancing accountability mechanisms

When road-building was in the hands of government, there were two problems. One was that decision-making was centralised and the other was that decisions were made by bureaucrats. This meant that in effect there was no way for local people to influence priorities or obtain improvements. Under the new arrangement people who use roads set priorities, know who to go to if there are problems with road maintenance, and can change those responsible if they are dissatisfied with their service.

Making social organising a critical activity

Usually road-building is conceived as a technical exercise of engineering and financing. In this case, these activities were complemented by social organising from the very beginning, with the assessment of villagers' interactions and ability to work together.

Rice production in the Philippines

Authors

Cesar Ledesma and Steve Waddell

Cesar Ledesma is Executive Director of Technical Assistance
Center for the Development of Rural and Urban Poor

Case type

Industry—rice

Location

Philippines

Sectoral context

In the Philippines NGOs are well developed, particularly with regard to working with poor and agrarian communities and environmental issues. There is also a sophisticated and internationally competitive business sector which includes both indigenous and foreign corporations. However, government development was hindered by decades of dictatorship which finally ended (in 1986) with the overthrow of President Marcos. Social dynamics are defined in large part by great inequity in wealth, with a few families controlling vast percentages of the most productive land and other assets.

Major participants

- Philippine Rice Research Institute (PhilRice)
- Dole Philippines (Dolefil)
- Technical Assistance Center for the Development of Rural and Urban Poor (TACDRUP)

Societal goal

- Achieving high rice yields while conserving land fertility

Civil society goal

- Enhancing the livelihood of small farmers
- Minimising the use of chemicals

Government goal

- Achieving food security
- Increasing exports
- Supporting agrarian land reform

Business goal

- Making contract growing viable
- Providing the Japanese market with high-quality rice

SLC product

The case began with a highly fractured approach to rice production which produced highly inequitable economic benefits and declining rice yields with low quality. It ends with an integrated approach of yields increasing in quality and quantity with more equitable economic benefits.

Description

In 1998 the Philippines imported one million metric tons of rice, making it the second biggest importer in the world. This followed implementation of green revolution technologies highly dependent on chemicals. After initially increasing yields, the chemicals produced decreasing yields, environmental and health problems and new, disease-resistant pests.

The Philippines government was tackling the issue of land reform by breaking up some large estates and plantations and allocating the land to small farmers. However, land distribution by itself did not prove successful. There were no technical development, sales, distribution and marketing structures to support the small farmers. They were not capable of meeting the demands of modern markets for consistent quality, competitive price, on-time and predictable delivery and bulk sales.

Given the seriousness of the problem it was not difficult to get positive responses to suggestions for change from the various sectors of society. However, the problem was that there was no unified approach to solving the problem. Each major player has its own individual initiative. The government focused on developing high-yielding varieties of rice, the business sector focused on efficiency and productivity and the NGOs focused on developing social structures and systems at the community level coupled with the introduction of appropriate technology for sustainable farming.

Traditionally the government, business corporations and NGOs looked on each other more as rivals than as partners in the arena of development. Between them relationships ranged from mild distrust to acute antagonism, depending on the issue. Each always had something to say against the other. And so, when one day in 1998 a government agency, a big business corporation and an NGO came together and agreed to form a partnership for rice production and marketing, only a few gave it a thumbs-up while many doubted its viability.

The government agency is the Philippine Rice Research Institute (PhilRice). It was established in 1985 and its major activities include: breeding high-yielding varieties of rice and making these available to seed growers and farmers; developing rice production technologies suited to the different growing conditions in the Philippines; and conducting seminars and training. It heavily promoted 'modern' agriculture techniques with disease- and pest-resistant varieties, and high use of chemicals for pest control and fertilisers. However, by the end of the 1990s declining yields and the advent of new pests and diseases forced a re-examination.

The big business corporation is Dole Philippines Incorporated (Dolefil), a subsidiary of the Dole Food Company, a US-based multinational corporation operating in 90 countries. Dolefil is a prime producer of fresh pineapple and banana for export. It has been operating in the Philippines since 1966 and now grows an area of more than 12,000 hectares. The company had attempted to expand from its core banana and pineapple plantation business to rice, but found the cost of production high and profits low.

The NGO is the Technical Assistance Center for the Development of Rural and Urban Poor (TACDRUP). Its major activities include community organising and co-operative development, sustainable agriculture and agro-forestry, micro-finance and community-based enterprises. It is a major advocate of organic farming because of environmental and farmer health and safety concerns and a view that dependence on expensive chemicals will produce lower incomes. TACDRUP is leading development of organic farming of rice. It also made an unsuccessful foray into rice processing.

These three parties created an unusual collaboration. Its creation did not come easily. In fact, it would not have come about if not for the efforts of Sylvia Ordonez, a woman who saw an opportunity for societal change as a challenge as well as an opportunity for a shift in the paradigm of development partnership in the Philippines. Ordonez is a feminist activist and a development leader in her own right. While director of the Technology and Livelihood Resource Center (a government-funded development institution) she met various leaders from different sectors in the development field. Ordonez relied on her friendship with the leaders of the three organisations to bring them together on several occasions over lunch or coffee to present her ideas. She persisted until she was able to facilitate an agreement.

At the same time that Ordonez was facilitating the co-operation of PhilRice, Dole Philippines and TACDRUP, a new President of the Philippines was elected. He renewed the government's intent to strengthen the agriculture sector and attain food security. This provided the impetus needed for the three organisations to jump into the water together.

Thus in October 1998 PhilRice, Dole Philippines and TACDRUP formally entered into a memorandum of agreement to undertake a joint venture. They combine their respective strengths, compensate the weaknesses of the other and bring together the goals of the three organisations in relation to rice production and distribution—profitability, productivity and social acceptability. The most important provisions in the terms of reference were the following:

1. PhilRice provides the quality foundation seed for distribution to accredited seed producers, who in turn produce certified seed that is distributed to farmers. In addition PhilRice provides training to the seed growers and monitors the production of quality seeds.

2. Dolefil buys the certified seed at a guaranteed floor price, cleans the seed and sells the seed to the farmers. Dole also buys the commercial rice produced by the farmers and markets the rice under its brand name.

3. TACDRUP organises and trains groups of rice farmers and facilitates the accessing of credit for rice production. It also supervises the milling and quality control of the certified seed and the commercial rice.

4. The economic benefits from the project are shared by the farmers, TACDRUP and Dole.

The farmers are able to augment their income by as much as 20% as a result of the price guarantee given by Dole. In real terms this translates to an increase from an average gross sales of 35,000 to 40,000 pesos per hectare to as much as 60,000 pesos per hectare. The project started with 200 hectares involving some 120 farmers. The average production per hectare ranges from four to five tonnes per harvest with two harvests a year. TACDRUP is also able to raise non-grant revenues by providing milling and warehousing services for Dole. And Dole makes its income from the sale of certified seed to the farmers. The greatest benefit for all participants is the sale of rice to the Japanese market. Previously, rice was not of sufficient quality to sell to the Japanese. The organic rice was well received.

SLC features

Leading by an intersectoral catalyst

Ordonez's role is widely recognised as critical for the initiative's success. She had credibility in the three sectors, and the ability to speak to their distinct needs.

Striking at the right moment

SLC initiatives arise from a mixture of crises, failure, new opportunities and vision. The initiative was proposed at a time when the general environment was right. Dole Philippines had learned it could not do rice production well, TACDRUP had developed organic rice production but was having trouble with processing and marketing, and there was a change in government with a President who wanted to demonstrate his commitment to the agricultural sector.

Identifying key competences

The parties all recognised that they could not do everything and that each had a particular competence. Dolefil's primary strength is recognised as marketing and sales, TACDRUP's is in organic rice production and the government's is in providing high-quality rice standards.

Developing shared vision and mutual commitment

The people involved were able to find a shared vision and common values including mutual respect and support for each other's objectives. This mutual respect provided the firm foundation for establishing a good working relationship and relating as equals.

Dividing tasks clearly

The tasks were clearly outlined in a memorandum of agreement. This clarity in responsibilities and recognition of the distinct goals provides a strong basis for mutual accountability.

Giving and risking rather than taking and playing safe

All the partners have more of a sense of giving rather than taking, although they all see the beneficial outcomes as clearly outweighing their costs. Each partner is taking a risk with respect to their distinct goals. This approach has facilitated the overcoming of differences.

Committing to learning and experimenting

Essentially the partners agreed to undertake an experiment collaboratively. None of them were sure the arrangement would work, and they had to commit to trying out their ideas in an atmosphere of mutual accountability and agreement.

Creating a systems approach to production

The new approach to rice production is a co-production approach among stakeholders. All parties involved in production are aware of one another and have collaboratively devised a new production system (as with the India CTD example, page 43). This contrasts to the traditional supply chain model where only direct suppliers and buyers are in contact with one another, or spoke-and-hub approaches where one organisation takes responsibility for organising all the others. The systems approach is grounded in mutual accountability, transparency and peer relationships.

Case name
Community-bank innovation in the US

Author
Steve Waddell

Case type
Community level—community development and banking

Location
Pittsburgh, USA

Sectoral context
In the United States in general the business sector is particularly powerful and well developed. Civil society is, in comparison to most countries, skilled in economic development and business-oriented issues. The case is an illustration of how government, civil society and business can work together.

Major participants

- Integra Bank
- Pittsburgh Community Reinvestment Group

Societal goal

- Civic economic development

Civil society goal

- Community development
- Non-discriminatory lending
- Access to market financial resources

Government goal

- Productive bank–community relationships

Business goal

- A supportive operating environment
- Profitable business
- Retailing banking development

SLC product

The bank and CBOs had a history of antagonism, with both operating independently. This was transformed into a joint development and delivery of banking products and services with important federal and local government support. This produced competitive profit returns for the bank, enhanced its market share, gave access to financial services to traditionally excluded people and enhanced the community's development.

Description

When two banks in Pittsburgh announced their merger, community activist Stanley Lowe saw an opportunity to create a new type of relationship with the new Integra Bank. The proposed merger would have to be approved by federal regulators who, among other things, would consider the community's concerns about the merger. In his role as head of the Pittsburgh Community Reinvestment Group (PCRG), Lowe wrote a letter to the merging banks that resulted in temporary withdrawal of the request for approval of the merger. 'They sent a cranky letter of demands,' recalls Don Reed, vice-president of community development for Integra. 'Certainly the threat was implied that if something didn't happen fast, the merger would be challenged.'

Gayland Cook, President of Integra Bank, Pittsburgh, recalls the situation as 'charged, but never antagonistic because the folks that represented the community groups were bringing things of value to the table'. Within three days a memorandum of understanding was negotiated, the merger proceeded and a most unusual bank–community relationship developed.

This occurred in Pittsburgh, a city of under 400,000 with a long and rich industrial history closely associated with steel. Since the 1950s de-industrialisation has turned the city into one that today is associated more often with universities and service industries. That transformation was parallelled with one that occurred in most large American cities where the white middle class moved to the suburbs and was replaced by low-income residents who were predominantly blacks and minorities.

Banks accompanied residents fleeing to the suburbs. Inner-city communities found themselves a source of deposits for a shrinking number of banks, without the investment opportunities. The practice of 'red-lining' by banks meant geographic lines were drawn around inner-city areas to designate them as ones where no lending would occur. The neighbourhoods became starved for mortgages and other lending, and their decline accelerated.

Under pressure from community activists, the federal government did two things that were critical to support change. They asked regulators to consider banks' community lending whenever the banks applied for expansion and closure of branches, mergers and acquisitions. This was operationally translated into giving communities a role in the public hearings that accompanied mergers, branch closures and openings. In addition, regulators rated banks on their community performance.

Second, the federal government obliged banks to make public information about their lending activity by geography and business line. This created a potential bridge for dialogue between the banks and community. Community activists could now make informed comments and suggestions, in contrast to their traditionally broad protests and suggestions that often reflected lack of understanding about banking.

In Pittsburgh the community also created an important innovation. Over 30 neighbourhood organisations joined together to form PCRG, which describes its mission as including, but not being limited to, 'promoting neighborhood reinvestment by financial institutions'. 'If you're a member, we hang together,' says Rick Swartz who heads a PCRG member organisation. 'If institutions feel they can buy off members with minuscule grants, the whole effort will collapse. If a group misses a certain number of meetings, you're excommunicated.'

The civic government also innovated. It created the Urban Redevelopment Authority (URA) with members including PCRG and banks. The URA creates Community Development Advisory Groups (CDAG) with each bank. Although most CDAGs meet with their bank counterparts quarterly, Integra meets monthly. This municipal government intervention is backed up with all of the government's tools and its influence over where government, hospitals and schools do their banking—a tool the government has made clear it will use as a carrot and stick.

The Integra CDAG meetings encompass a broad range of overlapping interests. The outcomes are summarised in a memorandum of understanding (MoU). Since the first MoU, a process of regular renegotiations developed an unusually comprehensive agreement that might be best likened to a written social contract, complete with renegotiation dates and processes. It defines parties as including specific bank and PCRG representatives. Staff support is provided by both PCRG and the bank. Meetings alternate in location between the bank and community organisations.

The MoU defines processes that led to Integra developing new bank products and delivery strategies by working directly with community organisations. For the communities this means that they can finally get access to the bank's financial services.

The relationship has revolutionised traditional bank approaches to retail low-income communities. Traditional connections were based on focus groups and surveys with people who have little knowledge about banking. This new process helps overcome the inherent difficulties for the bank in working with people with English as a second language and who are often not as articulate as traditional product development and marketing processes assume.

Through its CDAG, Integra and the communities have developed a process to continually develop and improve services and the community. One new strategy that has developed is reducing both loan defaults and the bank's costs to enforce the terms. Whereas banks traditionally resort to costly legal steps to enforce loans, the community organisations now act more as participants in a peer lending model by providing education (as opposed to marketing) with the products and support to get back on track if there are defaults. Banks, given their drive for profit maximisation, simply cannot develop the trust to be able to act in this way.

The MoU formalises a significant annual $55,000 commitment by Integra to PCRG, whose budget also includes substantial non-bank funds. By being formalised and funnelled through PCRG as part of a much larger budget, fears about co-optation of PCRG members is greatly reduced. The infrastructure supporting the relationship also includes government lending programmes targeting low-income communities. This is delivered through a bigger collaboration including Integra, PCRG, the Pittsburgh History and Landmarks Foundation (PH&L; devoted to historic preservation and actively supports community development), two non-profit centres that provide technical assistance to community organisations, the Pittsburgh Equity Fund (PEF) which raised money for affordable housing, and the Pittsburgh Partnership for Neighborhood Development (PPND; a non-profit agency that collects money from foundations, the city and banks to provide support for neighbourhood organisations).

SLC features

Aggregating community voice into a market force

PCRG has enough power to make banks realise that it is an organisation that they must deal with—something individual neighbourhood groups could not do for the whole city. For Integra, PCRG offers an attractive vehicle to interact with the community by aggregating its market so the bank does not have to negotiate with separate organisations.

Creating a multi-party forum

The CDAG is a critical innovation that functions with the presence, support and authority of the city, but in fact the principal parties are Integra and PCRG. By meeting monthly, in contrast to other bank–community CDAGs meeting quarterly, there is much more opportunity for continuity and development of a deep relationship based on mutual understanding and exploration of issues and opportunities.

Writing a formal definition of the relationship

Rather than be subject to the whims of a particular opportunity or events or leaving things loose, the MoU has elevated the relationship to one with a clear understanding of commitments and history (the MoU is also structured as an historical record).

Integrating various scales of change

The MoU development process allows the relationship to develop opportunities within a defined framework (first- and second-order change), while also creating planned moments for deeper re-evaluation (second- and third-order change).

Producing valued outcomes by all

Within six years of beginning the relationship, Integra counted 60% of people living in Pittsburgh as its clients. It achieved a substantial portfolio of loans, new products and new delivery channels. The communities substantially increased their access to personal loans and mortgages, loans to minority and female-owned small businesses, and commercial developments.

Uncovering assumptions for innovation

Banks presume that low-income markets are unprofitable. The Integra–PCRG demonstrated that such conclusions are based on assumptions such as that their products and delivery structures are appropriate. New products, delivery structures and loan repayment vehicles were among the innovations.

Building on geographic symmetry

Integra Bank has a geographic division that overlaps very substantially with the area of PCRG's members. This made for much more valuable and easier collaboration than was true for other banks.

Using dense social network ties

Although Integra, PCRG and its members are the focal relationship, there are dense personal and organisation networks to support them. PH&L, for example, was an important place where community activists and bankers met even before the CDAG relationships developed. The government federally and locally provides important support through legislation, their own networks and their buying power.

Case name
The Access Initiative/Partnership for Principle 10 for global environmental decision-making

Author

Steve Waddell

Case type

Global change

Location

Global

Sectoral context

The global arena following World War II was dominated by agreements between governments and inter-governmental organisations such as the United Nations and World Bank. However, the ability of governments to take effective global action is weak. Business is the strongest global actor. Its role has grown significantly since the late 1980s when the Soviet Union collapsed and governments started promoting international business as agents of development. Civil society is comparatively weak globally, in large part due to the fact that much of its strength arises from close relationship to communities and building close relationships globally is problematic.

Major participants

- World Resources Institute
- NGOs in Chile, Mexico, Hungary, Uganda, Thailand, Indonesia, South Africa, India and the US
- Governments in those countries to varying degrees and other countries (e.g. Sweden, UK, Italy, European Commission)
- World Bank, UNEP, UNDP, and IUCN

Societal goal

- Sustainability

Civil society goal

- Access to information, participation and justice in environmental decision-making

Government goal

- Strengthening national environmental and development systems, while respecting the rights of all

Business goal

- Business has not been involved to date

SLC product

International agreements that governments sign usually produce little change. Sometimes signatures are just a public relations gesture. Other times political will subsequently disappears. And sometimes governments simply do not understand how—or have the capacity—to follow through. The Access Initiative (TAI) is a novel approach of NGOs to address these problems of national-level implementation and give life to a particular commitment of governments in the Rio Declaration on Environment and Development. It has been influential in development by the United Nations of the concept of 'Type II' partnerships, which refer to partnerships among government and non-government actors that can help realise governments' international commitments.

Description

The 1992 Rio Earth Summit seemed like a watershed event at the time. It was the largest international meeting ever held on the environment. Heads of state were joined by over 10,000 NGO representatives who made their global presence felt. One commitment governments signed up to was the Rio Declaration on Environment and Development, which listed 27 principles.

However, the Declaration produced little change. At the turn of the millennium, Frances Seymour, Elena Petkova and others at the World Resources Institute (WRI) in Washington, DC, began talking about doing something about it. WRI, highly regarded internationally for the quality of its research, did not seem a likely leader to foment action on an international agreement. That type of work typically was associated with more direct-advocacy NGOs. However, Seymour and Petkova were concerned about governance and institution building. They circulated a paper about what they might do that would fit with their organisation's resources and competence. 'It was also an effort to link research more directly to action,' commented Petkova, 'to build a constituency and a user base before the research product was ready and thus get a research product that reflects user demand and needs.'

In the summer of 2000, Petkova shared their paper with Sandor Fulop of the Environmental Management and Law Association (EMLA), a comparatively small Hungarian NGO that focused on legal strategies concerning sustainability. Through discussions, Principle 10 of the Rio Declaration surfaced as one with particular strategic importance. Principle 10 reads:

> Environmental issues are best handled with participation of all concerned citizens, at the relevant level. At the national level, each individual shall have appropriate access to information concerning the environment that is held by public authorities, including information on hazardous materials and activities in their communities, and the opportunity to participate in decision-making processes. States shall facilitate and encourage public awareness and participation by making information widely available. Effective access to judicial and administrative proceedings, including redress and remedy, shall be provided.

Together EMLA and WRI hosted a meeting in November 2001 at WRI's offices with about 50 people, mainly from NGOs (but also from international government agencies) to further discuss their options. Enthusiastic support emerged for integrating serious science into development of a new global network with the goal of giving life to participatory practice in environmental decision-making. The key would be coming up with a common set of indicators of Principle 10 for application across diverse countries. The World Summit on Sustainable Development (WSSD) in Johannesburg in 2002 was a political opportunity to legitimise the initiative. Case studies would be conducted on the current state of Principle 10 application in enough countries to grab world attention. But rather than use them to follow a traditional advocacy route to then demanding government adherence, a more collaborative approach would be developed to engage governments more as colleagues in the project.

For this approach, governments that were positively disposed to the effort would be the best to engage. As Zehra Aydin-Zidos of the United Nations Commission on Sustainable Development commented: 'There is lots of resistance to bringing in other actors because [implementation of the Rio Declaration] is seen as a government domain.'

The original idea of identifying a single partner NGO in various countries changed when it became obvious that no NGOs possessed the three competences necessary to do all the necessary work in a country: competence in participatory practices, legal systems and writing of laws, and development of environmental indicators and measurement. Other competences emerged as important in specific locations, including competence in environmental education and journalism. Consequently, the idea of creating a collaboration of at least three NGOs at each country site emerged. This had the added benefit of enhancing legitimacy of, and disseminating knowledge about, the initiative.

At another organising meeting in February 2001, ideas were further developed and a core team began to emerge with organisations, in addition to WRI and EMLA, from Chile, Thailand and later Uganda. Determined to make the initiative sizable enough to grab world attention, Seymour and Petkova in particular focused on recruiting, making sure that partners not only had the competences but also that the goals of TAI fit well with their priorities and missions. By August partners in ten locations were identified: the American states of California and Ohio and, in addition, Hungary, Mexico, Chile, South Africa, Uganda, India, Indonesia and Thailand.

TAI was established as assessing and stimulating progress by governments at the national level on the:

- Legal framework for access to information
- Dissemination of information
- Practice of participation
- Accessibility of justice
- Capacity of the public to exercise their access rights

The NGOs set about assessing the legal frameworks and conducting case studies of how the above factors were addressed. For example, the Mexican team focused on the response to a volcano eruption; cases of a cholera outbreak and fish poisoning by chemicals were developed in Uganda; and a fire in a tyre dump was the focus in California. From 17 cases a methodology and benchmarks were established.

The way the tasks were undertaken was as important as completing them. An action research strategy both developed findings and engaged governments in the work. Governments' interest was piqued because they were expected to demonstrate what they had accomplished at the WSSD. However, as a network of NGOs TAI presented both an opportunity and a potential danger for bad exposure.

Interactions with national governments depended on a variety of factors, including the governments' priorities, personal relationships of people from the NGOs and the state of participatory practices. In Mexico with the newly elected Fox government, the initiative received a warm response, in part because of government priorities and in part because any criticism that arose in the case studies would reflect on the previous government. In Uganda the government was persuaded to take a positive position because, as Godber Tumushabe of the NGO ACODE (Advocates Coalition for Development and Environment) explained, he was 'able to convince government agencies that their involvement was aimed to help improve their performance'. As well, they were undoubtedly aware that although he 'preferred using the carrot, he [I] could use a stick.' The Thailand Environmental Institute was already working on governance and the environment; by engaging as an NGO partner an institute established by the Thai King, TAI had good senior government connections.

Despite Herculean efforts, funding was a chronic problem, and much of the work was done on a volunteer basis. The network only met four times before the WSSD, and it depended heavily on email and the Internet. However, the report was ready for delivery with the opening of WSSD on 23 August 2002.

The report and methodology represented only one part of the TAI effort. Over the year preceding the WSSD there were preparatory meetings around the world held by the United Nations. WSSD was originally designed as an event that would help spur governments to act on their 1992 commitments by highlighting their progress, and stimulate new commitments. However, reviews of governments' achievements revealed a dreary lack of progress. There was obviously a basic design flaw in the whole approach behind the international inter-governmental commitment and meeting strategy.

All the TAI NGOs promoted TAI through the preparatory meetings and the Commission for Sustainable Development (CSD)—the UN agency organising the WSSD. Looking for another strategy given the design flaw, the CSD concluded that organisations outside government should be brought in to help put pressure on governments to meet their commitments. These 'Type II' partnerships were presented also as a vehicle to obtain funding.

The TAI NGOs concluded that TAI must continue to be an independent civil society initiative that controlled application of the assessment methodology, for it to be a legitimate accountability mechanism. However, they decided to create a global framework for partnering with government that they called Partnership for Principle 10 (PP10). This would have three objectives:

1. Creating a global knowledge base, learning environment and a positively competitive environment for governments to improve their performance

2. Obtaining clear commitments from governments for action with respect to implementing Principle 10, and

3. Raising funds to do the work

In April 2003 the first global TAI meeting was held with government representatives to form PP10. Governments and NGOs from a dozen countries and four intergovernmental organisations participated in either TAI or the founding PP10 meeting. The scale of funding needed continued to be elusive, in part due to the complexity of government departments that must be engaged—environmental, foreign aid and foreign affairs.

Part of the problem was that, although most TAI NGOs were strongly supportive of PP10, NGOs in general were ambivalent about the idea of the Type II partnerships, for some good reasons. They were being asked to implement agreements that they had little role in defining and might well disagree with, and the Type II strategy raised the spectre of governments running away from obligations and shifting the burden to others. Governments of developing nations worried that foreign aid would shift from them to NGOs, and inappropriately legitimise the role of transnational corporations in international environmental governance.

Without greater NGO and government consensus, many saw the Type II partnership route as leading to unnecessary controversy. Moreover, many governments and NGOs view each other as adversaries rather than partners. Most European countries are involved in another initiative (Aarhus) which is complementary to TAI and therefore appears to some as a duplication.

Despite these challenges, the TAI NGOs remain enthusiastic and committed. A complex multi-pronged strategy for NGO–government relationships is emerging that reflects the idea that NGOs should be engaged directly in implementation of international agreements. It responds to criticism that international agreements are either so general as to be of little use or so specific that they cannot appropriately reflect global diversity.

Government–TAI commitments include funding and action to implement Principle 10. Three different structures are emerging to respond to the criticism and yet reflect the basic TAI idea:

1. Regional, legally binding initiatives (such as Aarhus) in the inter-governmental tradition

2. PPIO

3. Simple national government–TAI NGO relationships

TAI is expanding to include more countries, in response to significant interest by governments and NGOs. TAI's work with governments is evoking deeper engagement in response to its findings. In addition, TAI anticipates doing assessments on a regular two- or three-year basis and producing both national and global reports.

SLC features

Customised rather than roll-out strategies

A classic problem in global decision-making where national governments are the participants is the need to maintain the fiction that all governments are equal and that one process can fit all. TAI and PPIO are offering a way to have a global framework but develop very customised working processes that respond to a particular government's circumstances.

Focus upon the work rather than the structure

Both TAI and PPIO are evolving by doing work in response to a problem, and drawing lessons about how to organise the work based on their experiences. They have spent a minimal amount of time talking about structure in the abstract, and have avoided mistakes that could have resulted from designing their structures and processes with too much dependence on the experience of others.

Highly cost-effective development

By mid-2003 after two and a half years of development, the actual TAI–PPIO cash expenditures are less than $2 million. This is a minuscule amount of money when the product is considered: a global network well established in five countries with historic experience in another four jurisdictions and with significant expansion plans and potential; a global methodology grounded in solid empirical work; and assessments in nine jurisdictions and a synthesis based upon them.

Collaborative ownership

The decision by TAI to create partnerships among at least three NGOs in countries was a necessity that proved a virtue. In the four jurisdictions where this strategy was not pursued—rather, individual NGOs and contractual relationships with TAI were elected—the results were much less robust. The partnership strategy leveraged resources of more organisations (including volunteer ones) and a greater range of specialised resources, and created a collectively owned initiative culture that is a much stronger base for expansion and dissemination.

An action learning approach

Many SLC initiatives involve developing new knowledge in a traditional scientific sense. For example, a new assessment methodology was developed by TAI. However, the *way* the research was developed reflected the understanding that a new organisational structure as well as the methodology was needed. Producing scientific 'truths' is not sufficient for SLCs; they must be connected to implementation and application processes.

A focus on carrots and presence of sticks

Change processes involve both opportunities and threats. Some people and organisations are motivated principally by one, others by the other. To tap into the type of energy that is needed for the change work, the basic draw is a vision about how to make things better. A leading group of early adapters can develop this vision. However, the presence of sticks is also necessary, at least implicitly.

Chapter 4
What is changing?

There are four key systems in SLC: political, social, economic and environmental. At historic moments the alignment between these systems has shifted like a societal earthquake. For example, 1930s changes in the United States associated with the New Deal and in other Western countries with the rise of the welfare state marked a significant realignment in favour of the power of the political system. The end of the Soviet era marked a realignment in favour of both economic and social systems. The SLC cases described here are all part of a realignment in response to globalisation and environmental crises. At these historic moments the social contract is changed, and SLC initiatives are experiments to develop new social contract rules.

This SLC transformation includes change in values, behaviours, beliefs and structures. Rather than a negotiations-based change that re-divides a pie or makes incremental modifications, SLC is a re-visioning and reinventing process where different world-views, resources and weaknesses are brought together in an intimate transformative and synergistic way.

Core to this order of change is the ability of people and organisations to create new relationships. In all the case stories, learning resulted in amazing sustainable change that occurred by making unusual connections between:

- A bank and community-based organisations (CBOs)

- Forestry companies, environmentalists and aboriginal government

- Poor villagers, road-building companies, various government levels and a foreign donor agency

- Rural citizens, multinational and large corporate water construction companies and a CBO

- Senior civil servants, people from the economic elite, small farmers and poor women

- Civil society activists and corporate leaders around the world

- National governments and a global network of environmental, legal and participatory CBOs

Creating these new relationships raised awareness and revealed assumptions and a visionary common purpose and desire that was masked by traditional views and ways of working. Developing the relationships does not mean suppressing traditional individual and organisational objectives, but rather reconceiving them—

reorganising them to reach traditional objectives *and* reach new collective ones. Sustainable business can be profitable—but it has to take seriously the objective of sustainability as well as profits.

The diverse boundaries crossed in these new relationships are many. But they can usefully be summarised as boundaries of depth and of breadth. These were summarised in Table 1.1 in Chapter 1 and are presented diagrammatically in Figure 4.1 below. Successful SLC initiatives must address learning and change in *depth*— with each of individual, organisational, sectoral, societal and environmental system levels—and across the *breadth* of spiritual, mental, physical and emotional arche- types—the environmental, political, economic and social systems.

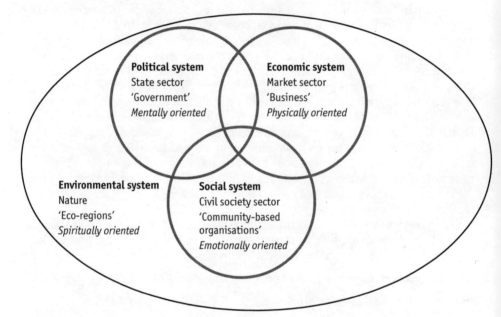

FIGURE 4.1 The four-sector model

A holistic systems model

This is a holistic systems model, which contrasts with most approaches to change. Those working with personal development and in heroic leadership traditions— common in the United States—focus on the role of the individual as the key agent of change. At its extreme, this tradition says that change simply requires people with the right awareness, values and skills. At the other end of the spectrum are people who focus on organisations, institutions and social structures ranging from businesses and business rules of the game to families as the critical agents for change. This latter tradition is particularly strong with sociologists and the organisational development school. Even the most marvellous individuals, says this tradition, will be thwarted in any change effort by larger forces embedded in social structures . . . after all, CEOs have to pay attention to market rules.

The SLC approach stresses that deep change requires not an either–or but a both–and approach. Large-scale change efforts depend on the learning and change abilities of individuals, groups, organisations and groups of similar organisations called *organisational sectors*. Individuals must approach deep change as a profoundly personal process where they will reflect on their own behaviours and values and how they have to change to address the challenge or develop the opportunity facing them—SLC is not successful if participants approach it simply as a process where other people must change. Similarly, organisations must be able to respond to the challenges and opportunities with a willingness to re-examine basic assumptions and to change in response to new findings.

In the bank example, the bankers and community activists had to individually reassess their traditional adversarial views and behaviours, and create new structures (the Community Development Advisory Group) and processes (jointly developing and delivering new products). Bankers had to overcome stereotypes of community representatives as economically ignorant and incompetent, and be willing to recognise that they had made some inaccurate assumptions—such as bank branches being the delivery structure and legal mechanisms being necessary for enforcement of loan agreements. Community groups had to overcome stereotypes about bankers being indifferent, and to be willing to accept that banks need to achieve a reasonable rate of profit.

At the societal level, SLC can be thought of as a process of realigning the relationship between the three core systems that make up human civilisation: the political, economic and social. Figure 4.1 represents these human systems as part of the larger system of the environmental.[1] In the banking system the environmental system was not a focus, but the case resulted in realignment of the way the other three systems interact—their relationships.

Although Figure 4.1 suggests that the three systems are equal in power, of course this is not true. Adapting the figure to the United States today would require a very large circle for the economic system; for China and Cuba the political system would be particularly large and the social system very small; in Bangladesh, where CBOs are very powerful, the social system might be the largest. In different cultures the figure would also show varying degrees of overlap of the circles. In the United States, the sectors are relatively separate in comparison to Europe where they are more integrated (Van Tulder 2003).

From this systems perspective, the Indian and Madagascar cases are examples of realignment of political system control of the economic development and road-building activities, respectively. In the GRI and TAI cases the economic and social systems are asserting their roles in creating a new global system that was traditionally the purview of the political system. In the Canadian forestry case the political system simply 'failed' to play its traditional role of arbitrator, and in the South

---

1   This model was developed by several people around the same time, including Sandra Waddock and L. David Brown.

African water case and the Philippine rice case the political system's power over infrastructure building and land reform proved insufficient to realise the desired results.

A key SLC concept: organisational sectors

The 'systems' are a bit abstract and the realignment is easier to see in terms of organisations that represent the systems. Governments collectively are referred to as the state organisational sector and make up the political system. Businesses are referred to as comprising the market sector and make up the economic system. Non-governmental, labour and religious organisations collectively make up the civil society sector and social system (Perlas 2000).[2] This does not mean, of course, that government and civil society organisations do not have an economic role—rather, it means that their distinctive role is stewardship and leadership of the political and social systems, respectively.

In the remaining chapters of this book we will focus on changing relationships at the organisational and sectoral levels. Thinking in terms of three systems represented by 'organisational sectors' of the state, the market and civil society is a critical concept for operationalising SLC. This allows aggregation of individuals and organisations to produce a powerful strategy for change. SLC is best undertaken with a good understanding about the distinct motivations and competences of the sectors and what they do for our society.

Why there are three sectors and not two, four or more is related to the observation that there are three types of individuals (emotionally, physically and mentally oriented) (Seagal and Horne 2000). The sectors can be thought of as organisational manifestations of differences between individual human beings. The sectors are groupings of organisations that share attributes and core logics. Promoting one sector at the expense of another is akin to suppressing one segment of society. Thinking of one sector as being fundamentally 'flawed' (as opposed to thinking the way the sector operates as flawed) is similar to thinking that a particular group of people is fundamentally flawed.

All the cases have been described in terms of the organisational sectors of the participants, because this helps explain what actually happened. Rather than thinking simply in terms of individual heroes and organisations, thinking in terms of sectors (clusters of similar people and organisations) helps understand the core dynamics at work. In the Indian case, the market and civil society sectors were strengthened to do some tasks either not being done before or being performed by the state. In the Philippine case, civil society was strengthened to support a market sector restructuring that shifted from privileging big enterprise to encouraging small enterprise. In the Canadian case a pitched battle between the market and civil society sectors, with the First Nations people as an important semi-state sector,

---

2   Nicanor Perlas refers to the 'cultural system' rather than social system. In the model here, culture is associated with the way the systems interact.

resulted in a new type of social contract to accommodate previously conflicting needs.

The names of the organisational sectors are often used rather loosely. A disciplined analysis defines their distinct attributes. Drawing from a large body of work, some of these are presented in Table 4.1. The attributes of each sector collectively define its distinctive *logic*. For example, 'non-profit' is not the defining characteristic that makes an organisation reflect a civil society logic—rather, it is just one of many. A large hospital may be legally non-profit, but in terms of other attributes it may be more like a business. Organisations can actually be rated for each attribute to determine how close they are to the organisational archetypes and how much they mix types.[3] Most organisations will score high on the attributes in one column.

	State sector	Market sector	Civil society sector
Primary concern	Political systems	Economic systems	Social systems
Control unit	Voters/rulers	Owners	Members
Primary power form	Laws, police, fines	Money	Traditions, values
Primary goals	Societal order	Wealth creation	Healthy communities
Assessment frame	Legality	Profitability	Justice
Goods produced	Public	Private	Group
Dominant organisational form	Governmental	For-profit	Non-profit
Operating frame	Administrative	Managerial	Developmental
Relationship basis	Rules	Transactions	Values
Temporal framework	Election cycles	Profit-reporting/ business cycles	Sustainability/ regeneration cycles

TABLE 4.1 Some comparative distinctive attributes of the sectors

Sources: Brown and Korten 1991; Etzioni 1961; Najam 1996; Nerfin 1986; Ouchi 1980; Thompson *et al.* 1991; Williamson 1981; Wuthnow 1991

Understanding these differences is critical for bringing together organisations from the sectors. Those involved in the banking case had to be responsive to all three temporal frameworks to get the support of the participants in the collaboration. It was critical to integrate production of new housing units—breaking ground and opening new centres—into the election cycles and political photo opportunities; the bank had to make competitive profits within a time period that made sense for their investors; and the housing had to be sustainable for the community members so they could financially afford it and physically maintain it.

---

3   This is a very useful thing to do when assessing potential partners in a collaboration.

The sectors have distinct operating frames. The administrative logic of government expresses itself with a focus on development and application of rules; the managerial logic of business emphasises the goals, and rewards entrepreneurial ways of achieving them; the development logic of civil society means that it is important to have highly participatory processes to identify the goals and how to achieve them. SLC initiatives must be able to integrate these different ways of organising work. This is obvious with TAI, for example, with its CBO focus on promoting participatory processes and influencing governments' administrative and regulatory strategies to accommodate these.

	State	Market	Civil society
Resources	• Regulatory and taxation powers	• Capital and financial assets	• Inspirational and volunteer assets
	• Enforcement networks	• Production networks	• Community networks
	• Policy impact knowledge	• Specialised industry knowledge	• Specialised community/ issue knowledge
	• Government reputation	• Business reputation	• Community reputation
	• Administrators	• Entrepreneurs	• Community developers
Weaknesses	• Inflexibility in rule application	• Tendency to monopoly	• Restricted/ fragmented interest focus
	• Slow decision-making	• Disregard for externalities	• Amateurism
	• Complexity of jurisdictions/levels	• Poor integration of long-term concerns	• Material scarcity
	• Difficulty in internal co-ordination	• Inequality of outcomes	• Difficulty in achieving large scale
	• Desire to control other sectors	• Ideological ignorance/ transactional parochialism	• Ideological parochialism (political correctness)
	• Partisan-driven posturing	• Shareholder fixation	• Weak economic understanding

TABLE 4.2 Sectors' generic comparative primary resources and weaknesses

The distinctive attributes are the source of the distinct resources and weaknesses of the sectors, some of which are presented in Table 4.2. All sectors can possess all the resources and weaknesses to some degree. However, some tend to be more dominant in one sector. For example, the companies participating in GRI have substantial business reputations that have a trust dimension, but there is simply not enough trust between them and the general public to do the work on their own that GRI is doing—indeed, this is the very criticism that is likely to make the business-led environmental framework ISO 14000 less powerful. Civil society organisations have greater community trust because when well organised their goals are literally the same as those of their communities—whereas businesses always have a profit-making goal.

Talking about things that an organisation does inherently badly is not as easy to discuss as things that an organisation does well, but they are nevertheless just as important to recognise. The weaknesses identified here draw on concepts of 'market failures', 'externalities' and from authors writing about the public sector and non-profits (Brown and Kalegaonkar 1998; Bruyn 1991, 2000; Cowen 1988; Henderson 1991; Lutz and Lux 1988).

Market-sector solutions are often criticised for creating winners and losers—a phenomenon explained by systems analysis as the tendency for 'success to go to the successful'. In addition, disregard for externalities as seen with businesses' environmental damage has spurred the development of the environmental movement. The state's role as rule-maker also generates the problem of 'red tape' and slow decision-making. Governments tend to think they know best and try to control the other two sectors. And although civil society is good at critiquing and community capacity-building, its community-based quality is one reason that it is poor at marshalling large resources on the scale of business or government.

	State	**Market**	**Civil society**
Capabilities	● Public policy development	● Production process management	● Issue development
	● Rule enforcement	● Capital mobilisation/ management	● Community organising
	● Government agency networks	● Business networks	● Civil society networks
Core competences	● Administering	● Managing	● Developing
	● Rules-focused activity	● Efficiency-focused activity	● Human impact-focused activity
	● Creation of 'level playing field'	● Profit generation	● Community trust generation
	● Redistribution of benefits	● Delivery of goods and services to medium and upper income	● Support for the vulnerable and marginalised
	● Standardised production	● Commercial production	● Artistic production

TABLE 4.3 Sectors' generic comparative primary capabilities and competences

The resources give rise to capabilities and core competences. Some of these are presented in Table 4.3 as generic sectoral distinctions, and therefore quite abstract. For any particular organisation they can be defined more specifically. For example, the Indian economic development initiative has established several CBOs to provide a safe place for parties diverse in power and culture to work together—something the competitive business structures and rules-based government structures cannot do as easily.

In the US bank case, the core competences of all the sectors come out. The government created the legislative right rules of the game for the relationship to develop. The rules encourage development of the bank–community relationship and provision of information about bank lending. The communities are most forcefully represented by CBOs, rather than local government. Of course the CBOs understood little about banking and the banks understood little about the communities—although both postured otherwise. After years of fighting, some bankers such as those in Pittsburgh decided to actually listen to the community groups. Those that have successful community banking strategies with profit rates similar to those for other business lines[4] learned three things: that they had the wrong delivery structure (branches, which are too costly), the wrong products (aimed for middle-income groups), and that the community organisations could actually play a key role in the development and delivery of profitable products. For low-income communities the CBOs helped transform business products into those containing greater human-focused impact value.

The rice example is accompanied by government support for land reform, based largely on arguments about equity. Land reform also reflects a free-enterprise perspective that suggests farmers owning their own land will be more productive than large absentee landowners with plantations. However, such farmers need a particular kind of production system—land reform on its own will not produce the improvements desired. Nor do most small farmers have the skills and expertise needed in today's complex global markets. These are now being provided by the CBO working with the farmer, which has particular expertise around farming issues and the trust of the farmers. The CBO has organised the farmers to aggregate them into a unit whose production level is of interest to a large corporation such as Dole, whose core competences are in its marketing and distribution.

The generalities of the core competences analysis can be made more specific by considering four other factors in developing intersectoral collaborations. These are presented in Table 4.4, which expands on work by Ostrom (Ostrom and Davis 1993).

The first factor—client-sector goal congruency—asks whether the organisation providing the service and the person receiving it have the same goals. In classic business cases there is low congruency because business wants to optimise price whereas customers want to minimise it—the true source of 'distrust' of the business sector. CBOs typically have high congruency—the CBOs in the cases aim to articulate the interests of communities through empowered processes. Government has medium congruency, since it needs to both manage tax levels and costs for the activities, and support attainment of the goals of citizens.

'Output specificity' refers to the ability to define the characteristics of a product or activity. Business works best when the characteristics are easily defined. In the South African case, business was in charge of construction where earth to be moved was measured in cubic metres and the lengths of pipe to be laid can be estimated

---

4   This includes most of the largest banks in the US.

	Government	Business	CBO
Client-sector goal congruency	Medium	Low	High
Output specificity	Medium	High	Low
Scale	Medium–large	Small–medium–large	Small–medium
Risk	Very low to very high	Low to high	Low

TABLE 4.4 Situational factors determining organisational appropriateness

quite accurately. CBOs are good for working in very low-specificity situations where there is poor definition of the outcomes such as with the TAI and 'community empowerment'. Government is best when there is medium specificity, such as providing supportive banking legislation and public funding, such as that provided by the United Nations Environmental Programme for the GRI. (Note that government often asks for too much specific detailed information, partly out of its desire to control other sectors. This was the case in South Africa where it insisted on highly detailed pricing which produced such large profits for the companies—the opposite of the intended effect—that the companies voluntarily returned money.)

'Scale' refers to the size of an initiative that the sector works with best. Business is extremely flexible in scale, although small business has many civil society attributes as well. Civil society, due to its need to maintain contact with quite specific communities, has difficulty operating at a very large level effectively. Government, because of its rule-oriented behaviour with generic public policy, has difficulty addressing specialised needs; however, it has the resources and networks to undertake substantial scale.

The fourth factor, risk, is something the market sector prides itself in measuring and working with. However, the risk premium that business would charge for working with the poor is usually prohibitive because of its high transaction costs. CBOs, because of the trust and knowledge they have in working with communities, have much lower transaction costs (a key insight behind micro-finance). The cases reflect that, in many situations, with proper resources CBOs can be better agents than government, and government's role is often in producing the right enabling environment and funding support.

The challenge of organisational change

Perhaps the greatest challenge in SLC initiatives is to bring about third-order change in the participating organisations. Often only small and relatively marginal parts of companies and governments are involved in the initiatives. They develop a specialised ability to participate in the initiatives, but that new operating style usually does not permeate to the rest of the organisation.

Among the cases, only the GRI represents an SLC that is designed to change the way the whole business organisation does its work. However, in the US banking case, retail banking was such an important part of the bank's market that the change was relatively profound. In the Canadian forestry case, activities ranging from marketing to forest harvesting techniques were changed.

Many times in SLC initiatives there is a significant shift in a business's definition of its business. In the Philippines case, DoleFil got out of the business of growing rice to focus on marketing and distribution of a new product—high-quality organic rice. In Madagascar the companies shifted from being road-builders to being trainers of local communities in road-building. In South Africa companies shifted from being construction companies to being co-producers of sustainable water systems.

Governments change from being direct doers to supporters. They got out of the water system building business in South Africa and reduced their direct economic development activity in India. In the Canadian forestry example they shifted from being arbitrators to being facilitators. The TAI model promotes government shifting from being in control to creating processes where citizens can take leadership.

Since CBOs are smaller, the impact of SLCs is often more substantial. Mvula Trust traditionally would have built the whole water system, and with Amanz'abantu it shifted to focus on institutional development. The Canadian environmental CBOs and the US community development CBO shifted from being critics to being active in education and marketing of products they helped design.

The role of the individual

All of this is well and good for the macro level, but where do individuals fit in? The distinctions of mentally, physically and emotionally centred individuals are drawn from Sandra Seagal's concept of human dynamics, 'a body of work based on investigations undertaken since 1970, involving more than 40,000 people representing over 25 cultures. It identifies and documents inherent distinctions . . . in human functioning [that] are more fundamental than age, race, culture, or gender' (Senge 2000).

Human dynamics, like SLC, is fundamentally a *systems* approach, but at the individual level. Rather than being a typology, human dynamics describes fundamental structures that are 'hard-wired' in people and approaches them as 'whole systems' to describe their associated processes and functions. Mental, emotional and physical 'are basic threads in the human system so fundamental and universal that we have termed them *principles*,' the authors explain (Seagal and Horne 2000). These are further described in Table 4.5. The threads combine in different ways, and Seagal has found that nine combinations account for 99.9% of individuals. All have a dominant principle that is referred to as a person's 'central principle' and describes *how* a person processes information and a secondary principle that determines *what* a person processes.

	Mental	Physical	Emotional
Emphases	Concepts, structures, ideas	Action, operations	Relationships, organisation
Process	Linear, logical, sequential	Systemic (by a comprehensive process of gathering, linking and seeing the interconnections among relevant data)	Lateral (by emotional association rather than logical connection)
Functions	• Thinking • Envisioning • Planning • Focusing • Directing • Creating structure • Seeing the overview • Establishing values, principles • Maintaining objectivity • Conceptualising • Analysing	• Doing • Making • Producing • Concretising • Detailing • Making operational • Utilising • Ensuring practicality • Co-operating • Synthesising • Systematising	• Feeling • Connecting • Communicating • Relating • Personalising • Empathising • Organising • Harmonising • Processing • Imagining

TABLE 4.5 Individual archetypes

Source: Seagal and Horne 2000

Mental	State	Physical	Market	Emotional	Civil society
Establishing values, principles	Rules-focused activity	Doing	Efficiency-focused activity	Feeling	Human impact-focused activity
Creating structure	Creating level playing field	Actualising	Profit generation	Relating	Community trust
Seeing the overview	Redistribution of benefits	Making	Delivery of goods and services to medium and upper income	Empathising	Support for the marginalised
Directing	Administering	Producing	Managing	Processing	Developing
Creating structure	Standardised production	System	Commercial production	Creative imagination	Artistic production

TABLE 4.6 Comparison of individual functions and sectoral competences

Tying this into the organisational, sectoral and societal levels suggests that the competences are organisational manifestations of the basic types of human beings. That is to say, we have produced these three different ways of creating organisations and the three basic types of systems in response to the three basic principles guiding our make-up as humans. To further make this connection, in Table 4.6 Seagal's functions are compared with the sectoral competences.

Therefore, the SLC challenge at the individual level is to develop the ability of individuals to understand the world from the vantage point of distinct logics and work together well. Seagal has worked with the Swedish government to integrate this development capacity into its education system. People must be able to appreciate the world-view of others who have a different basic principle. Often this requires that individuals move to a higher individual 'development stage'. These types of people are at a 'strategist' and 'magician' level of development according to one description, in contrast to 'opportunists', 'diplomats' and 'technicians' who can only see the world from their own viewpoint (Fisher *et al.* 2003).

Learning and change across levels

Although SLC focuses on societal-level change, achieving this level of change involves generating change within and between individuals, organisations and organisational sectors. Just as organisational learning involves individual learning, group learning and the ability to realign internal organisational boundaries (divisions, ministries, departments, units), so too SLC requires learning and change among the parts that make up society.

For example, with the GRI it is not sufficient for the individuals to learn more about measurement as individual learners or researchers. They have to integrate that knowledge into the way the businesses using the measures actually work. The goal is not just for the businesses to measures, but also to respond to the knowledge that measures represent. This means changing reward systems for employees, and very often the way a product is produced or a service is delivered. In the Canadian forestry case, employees of the companies, CBOs and First Nations people had to first learn about one another as individuals, before they could begin changing their organisations' relationships.

Of course important change can occur within a sector, which is the traditional focus of techno-fix responses to environmental crisis. However, people working within a sector are often limited by unrecognised assumptions that are revealed once they are challenge by different world-views. Typically techno-fixes in response to environmental issues are undertaken by people within business as they learn in traditional ways. The learning and potential change among individuals is increased when they work cross-sectorally. However, this is a necessary but not sufficient condition to bring about the scale of change that is needed to respond to the crises and visions that have driven the cases. The critical insight behind TAI is that to achieve sustainability requires basic change in the way individuals in government and CBOs interact. They had to move from seeing each other as adversaries to seeing each other as possessing complementary competences. That learning is then taken back to the participants' organisations to create broader change.

Often the challenge of integrating across depth and breadth of SLC shows up in hiring dilemmas. For example, in community banking in the US, a common question is whether someone who is a good banker (and tends to be physically centred) should be employed and taught to work with communities, or whether a good community activist (who tends to be emotionally centred) should be employed and trained in banking. This dilemma emphasises the importance of building team capacity to work across these systems.

References

Brown, L.D., and A. Kalegaonkar (1998) *Addressing Civil Society's Challenges: Support Organisations as Emerging Institutions*. Vol. XV (Boston, MA: Institute for Development Research).

—— and D.C. Korten (1991) 'Working More Effectively with Nongovernmental Organizations', in S. Paul and A. Israel (eds.), *Nongovernmental Organizations and the World Bank* (Washington, DC: World Bank): 44-93.

Bruyn, S. (1991) *A Future for the American Economy: The Social Market* (Stanford, CA: Stanford University Press).

—— (2000) *A Civil Economy* (Ann Arbor, MI: University of Michigan Press).

Cowen, T. (1988) 'Public Goods and Externalities: Old and New Perspectives', in T. Cowen (ed.), *The Theory of Market Failure: A Critical Examination* (Fairfax, VA: George Mason University Press).

Etzioni, A. (1961) *A Comparative Analysis of Complex Organizations* (New York: The Free Press).

Fisher, D., D. Rooke and W. Torbert (2003) *Personal and Organizational Transformations: Through Action Enquiry* (Boston, MA: Edge/Work Press).

Henderson, H. (1991) *Paradigms in Progress* (Indianapolis, IN: Knowledge Systems).

Lutz, M.A., and K. Lux (1988) *Humanistic Economics* (New York: Bootstrap Press).

Najam, A. (1996) 'Understanding the Third Sector: Revisiting the Prince, the Merchant and the Citizen', *Nonprofit Management and Leadership* 7: 203-19.

Nerfin, M. (1986) 'Neither Prince no Merchant: Citizen—An Introduction to the Third System', in K. Ahooja-Patel, A.G. Drabek and M. Nerfin (eds.), *World Economy in Transition* (Oxford, UK: Pergamon Press).

Ostrom, E., and G. Davis (1993) 'Nonprofit Organizations as Alternatives and Complements in a Mixed Economy', in D.C. Hammack and D. Young (eds.), *Nonprofit Organizations in a Market Economy* (San Francisco: Jossey-Bass): 23-56.

Ouchi, W.G. (1980) 'Markets, Bureaucracies and Clans', *Administrative Science Quarterly* 25: 129-41.

Perlas, N. (2000) *Shaping Globalization: Civil Society, Cultural Power and Threefolding* (Quezon City, Philippines: Center for Alternative Development Initiatives).

Seagal, S., and D. Horne (2000) *Human Dynamics: A New Framework for Understanding People and Realizing the Potential in our Organizations* (Waltham, MA: Pegasus Communications).

Senge, P. (2000) 'Forward', in S. Seagal and D. Horne (eds.), *A New Framework for Understanding People and Realizing the Potential in our Organizations* (Waltham, MA: Pegasus Communications).

Thompson, G., J. Frances, R. Levacic and J. Mitchell (1991) *Markets, Hierarchies and Networks: The Coordination of Social Life* (Newbury Park, CA: Sage Publications).

Van Tulder, R. (2003) Presentation at the 2003 Annual Meeting of the International Association for Business and Society, Rotterdam/Amsterdam.

Williamson, O. (1981) 'The Economies of Organization: The Transaction Cost Approach', *American Journal of Sociology* 87: 548-77.

Wuthnow, R. (1991) *Between States and Markets: The Voluntary Sector in Comparative Perspective* (Princeton, NJ: Princeton University Press).

Chapter 5
What are the change rationales and motivations?

People, organisations, sectors and society are all resistant to change. Continuing with the status quo takes less effort than changing. So why did businesses, governments and CBOs get involved in the examples of SLC? There are two basic reasons: they are pushed by crises and changes outside their control that make the status quo untenable, or they are attracted to envisioned opportunities about how things can be made better. Predictably, these motivations are often intertwined in any SLC initiative and the initial motivations and sustaining forces differ by societal system. Understanding the motivations and change dynamics at the sectoral and organisational levels is critical to creating a successful SLC initiative. A basic change strategy is to 'ride' these forces and design change processes to reflect them.

	State	Market	Civil society
Goal	Societal order	Wealth creation	Healthy communities
Destabilising forces	Globalisation Citizen pressure	Information and other hard technology Market competition	Organising technologies Changing relationships
Intersectoral imperative	Issue complexity	Sustainability	Social capital creation
SLC rationale	Combine the unique strengths and assets of each sector and offset their weaknesses to optimise societal outcomes		

TABLE 5.1 The societal learning and change challenge matrix: the big change dynamics by sector

The sectoral change dynamics

We can begin by returning to the distinct sectoral goals and expanding the SLC challenge matrix that was described in Chapters 1 and 4. Table 5.1 suggests that for each sector there are some macro forces that lead to change. These are described as destabilising forces—which means the forces that make the status quo untenable—and as intersectoral imperatives—which refers to why an intersectoral (SLC) approach is chosen as opposed to a single-sector solution.

The government imperatives

For governments, the goal is described as societal order. Governments are responsible for establishing laws and maintaining order, and a significant breakdown in societal order inevitably leads to change in government. Maintaining order and changing laws are obvious issues in the Canadian case, which involved the greatest civil disobedience in Canadian history, and the Madagascar case where the roads were so inadequate that banditry was rife. The cases in both the Philippines and South Africa were preceded by significant government change—from a dictatorship in the one case and apartheid rule in the other. The cases were part of the governments' activities to reorganise their countries. 'Reorganising' is also a key feature of government involvement in the other cases.

The two macro forces that are destabilising for government are citizen pressure and globalisation. Citizen pressure is the force most often associated with government action, and this was a major factor in the US banking, Canadian forestry, Indian economic development, Philippine rice and Madagascar road-building cases.

However, another powerful destabilising force for government is the vastly increased pace of global economic interaction and communication, magnified both by the fall of the Soviet system and the growth in information technology. This has led to a substantial reduction in the ability of governments to control and direct activities within their borders. Both the threat of flight by capital and business and the permeability of borders by media and people make national boundaries of decreasing importance and indicate that a new approach to governance is necessary. These factors are particularly evident in the GRI and TAI cases, but global opinion also had a big impact in the Canadian case through the European boycott of forest products.

In part because of this trend, there is increasing pressure for government to work with business and civil society in new ways. Many issues often relegated to be the responsibility of government directly or through regulation—healthcare, education, utilities, transportation infrastructure—are increasingly complex. Certainly the environment and economic development are two other issues that increasingly demand multi-stakeholder solutions. The government cannot effectively act on its own or even as an undisputed controller as it did in the past. Therefore intersectoral solutions are increasingly needed.

The business imperatives

For business the goal is wealth creation and the success of projects is determined by their profitability. This orientation makes business much more opportunity-driven than government. Major destabilising forces come through market competition as threat and technological innovation as opportunity. Both of these conspire to make business much more globally oriented. The India case is entirely organised around technological change which makes it attractive for business; in the Canadian case boycotts created a competitive threat; in the Philippines, South African, US and Madagascar cases new businesses were developed; and in the GRI example businesses are participating in large part to develop a uniform measurement technology.

But there is increasing business interaction with government and in particular civil society because of growing demands for business impacts to be more closely aligned with social and environmental concerns—in short, sustainability. The Canadian forest and GRI cases provide the most obvious examples of this. However, the bank case was in response to concerns about social equity and access to finance; in the Philippine case both income equity and use of chemicals in rice production were important factors; and in the India, Madagascar and South African cases economic equity and access to basic services were key factors and environmental concerns were secondary.

The civil society imperatives

For CBOs as the emotionally centred part of our organisational systems the forces are more ethereal. The goal is healthy communities—that is, health defined in terms of the particular geographic or issue community that the CBO represents. This goal and the cases suggest that the destabilising forces are new ways of organising and changing relationships. Since the end of the Cold War both individual and increasingly collective human rights are more broadly accepted as providing a basic foundation for the way we interact. This contrasts with the simple tradition of 'might is right'. This shift leads to new and more sophisticated processes for dialogue and 'large systems interventions' where diverse people come together to collectively plan their futures. The physical communications technologies such as email, e-conferencing and telephone provide important support for these new relationship-building approaches.

Literally every case features CBOs as collaborators to improve the health of their communities. Also in every case the CBOs moved from a position of hostility towards the market sector to one of collaborating with it, except in India and Madagascar where entirely new CBOs were created and in TAI where the market sector is not involved. In all cases CBOs participate in new intersectoral organisations that were created as a new type of collaboration CBO. The success of the participating CBOs in all the cases arose from the ability to create more powerful dialogue processes than traditionally had been possible.

For CBOs these relationships arise from broader understanding of the importance of social capital formation in our societal development. From the end of World War II until the 1980s government was seen as the lead agent in societal development. Since then business has been on the ascendant to replace it. However, there is increasing appreciation that civil society also has a critical role in building the type of society preferred by most people.

In the featured cases the role of CBOs is perhaps the most innovative. Having them involved in developing GRI's corporate reporting framework, supporting governments to achieve international commitments through TAI, working with forest companies to develop harvesting plans and technologies, and engaging CBOs in developing and delivering financial services, water, roads and economic initiatives all represent quite novel roles for the civil society sector.

The SLC rationale

From the perspective of societal and SLC design, breaking down the logics of the sectors (Chapter 4) suggests that the core rationale for creating intersectoral initiatives is to achieve outcomes that integrate the distinct logics of the sectors. For example, the sectors have different ways of assessing whether or not an outcome is 'good'. Can intersectoral collaborations significantly improve on non-collaboration outcomes to improve legality, profitability and justice? This is, it can be argued, the outcome of the cases presented here.

Legal frameworks were improved to make the outcomes possible: in the US, this took the form of the Community Reinvestment Act (CRA) and improvements to it in 1989; in South Africa legislation decentralised water jurisdiction; in the Philippines the government agriculture agency deferred its traditional role to the CBO; and GRI aims to overcome limitations of reporting frameworks that are constrained by national boundaries.

In the banking, water systems and rice cases the outcomes are certainly profitable; in the GRI example profitability is not really a factor (although cutting costs of the competing standards that would arise without a uniform measure is financially beneficial). And from the communities' perspectives, in all cases the outcomes are more 'just' since in the US they have improved access to development finance, in the Philippines the farmers are linked to a market to give them better prices, in South Africa poor rural communities have improved access to water and with GRI the triple-bottom-line focus aims to improve economic, environmental and social outcomes.

The attributes analysis of Chapter 4 suggests that strategies to attain sustainable development will probably involve intersectoral collaborations such as in South Africa with Mvula Trust. In that example the corporate logic is oriented towards a profit-cycle time-frame and that of government towards electoral cycles, but civil society is much more concerned with longer-term sustainability. This concern arises from a focus on community well-being. The product is a water system that is soundly engineered and constructed, takes into account natural environmental impacts and is maintained through fostering users' commitment to pay for the services and their ability to run maintenance organisations. This is a far cry from the well-known stories of millions of dollars of infrastructure in developing countries falling into disrepair within months of completion.

The logics also suggest substantial challenges managerially. Addressing only one or two of the time-frames, for example, is not sufficient. In the South African example, these forces are evident with the President's imperative that he unveil a new water system as part of his election campaign, businesses' insistence on competitive rates of return, and Mvula Trust's emphasis on user control of the water system.

The sectoral attributes analysis explains the core operational challenge as successfully integrating three distinct operating frameworks. Collaborations must somehow be responsive to the administrative logics of government that focus on application of rules and regulations, the developmental logics of civil society that emphasise broad participation, and managerial logics of business that set aggressive objectives and define success by achievement of these aims. In the cases, these differences typically resulted in business frustration over the slow pace due to government's multi-layered approval processes and CBOs' consensus-building.

Intersectoral collaborations, through their diverse membership, allow mitigation of the impact of externalities that are associated with business-alone approaches. This is part of the core goal of GRI with its development of a triple-bottom-line reporting framework; in the banking example, the trend for banks to withdraw and cause community decay is transformed; in the rice case environmental damage is reduced as farmers concerned about their own health work with the CBO to reduce chemicals; and in the South African case requirements to hire local people (in which the CBO plays a critical role) ensure that skills are developed and wealth is shared more broadly.

The cases provide good examples of integration that offsets sectors' weaknesses and combines their strengths. In the bank case, communities gain access to a financial system and the banks access the communities' trust networks and knowledge about how to work with the poor; and in the rice case communities gain access to the international marketing system and Dole accesses the CBO farmer network. In the South African water system case, earlier government-led attempts failed in part because of what was referred to as a '21 step, 21 month' red-tape approval process to get anything done. This provided an impetus commonly seen behind privatisations, to have business and CBOs take over the work. And, although volunteer resources were not significant in the South African case, in many other infrastructure projects they have cut costs by up to 90% to make many more projects possible—and create work for businesses in the process (Khan 1997; Plummer and Waddell 2002).

A unifying rationale

The unifying rationale for participation in SLC ventures is for participants to come together to do what they could not do on their own. SLC initiatives are complex and time-consuming, and if there is a way to achieve a goal without going through an intersectoral collaboration, it should be pursued. However, all the cases have one thing in common: they follow the failure of other approaches. Dolefil tried unsuccessfully to build a profitable rice-growing business, and its CBO partner TACDRUP tried unsuccessfully to get into the rice-processing business. They needed each other. In South Africa and other Southern countries there are many examples of expensive water infrastructure being built only to have it fall into disrepair within months. A CBO such as Mvula Trust, which was able to build communities' participation and capacity to be active in developing and maintaining the water system, was critical. Banks in the US had correctly concluded that they could not make a profitable business out of lending to low-income communities without the active participation of both government and CBOs.

Government	Business	CBOs
• Provide ways to increase effectiveness of public service provision *and* accountability (if right system created!) • Reduce direct involvement in rule enforcement while increasing its effectiveness • Improve welfare • Provide infrastructure	• Expand markets • Ensure supplies • Develop new products • Lower production and delivery costs • Expand investments • Improve human resources • Build support for local activity • Improve quality, regularity	• Increase access of the poor to goods and services • Provide new economic opportunities • Improve basic medical, education and health • Reduce environmental impact • Strengthen local cultures • Social cohesion

TABLE 5.2 Potential mutual-gain outcomes of business–government–CBO relationships

By joining together, the parties combine the unique strengths and assets of each sector and offset their weaknesses to optimise societal outcomes. Some of the mutual-gain outcomes are summarised in Table 5.2. These can be seen in all the cases. In India the Centre for Technology Development is successfully transferring technology from public scientific institutions to improve welfare and change the traditional approach of state-centric development strategies with collaborations. Through it businesses are developing new products and non-profits are enhancing opportunities for the traditionally marginalised such as the AWAKE women's micro-enterprise development CBO. In the Canadian forestry example the companies, CBOs and First Nations did most of the heavy lifting and thereby resolved a big problem for the government; the forest companies ensured long-term supplies; and the environmentalists ensured vastly reduced negative environmental impacts. And in Madagascar, government's role in road-building shifted from a direct road-building responsibility to simply funding road-building; moreover, revenues for the project were enhanced through tolls and costs were significantly cut through reduction in corruption and use of the labour of road users. For the villages it meant provision of a traditional public good.

Business motivations

These sectoral-level change forces have their counterparts for business at the organisational level. A global study for the International Youth Foundation in 2001 revealed five distinct answers to the question 'What motivates a business to become involved in youth employment issues?' (Waddell 2001). The findings provide a framework to understand what motivates a business to become involved in an inter-sectoral initiative more generally, as shown in Table 5.3.[1]

	Philanthropy	**(C)SR**	**CC**	**Mutual gain**	**SLC**
Stakeholder centricism	Corporate-centric	Corporate-centric	Corporate-centric	Opportunity problem-centric	Issue-centric
Corporate relation	Incidental	Peripheral	Strategic	Operational	Strategic-visionary
Relational systems	Gift	Obligations	Rights and responsibilities	Exchange	Common good
Power ethos	Business: +++ Gvt: + CS: +	Business: +++ Gvt: ++ CS: ++	Business: +++ Gvt: +++ CS: ++	Business: ++ Gvt: ++ CS: ++	Business: +++ Gvt: +++ CS: +++
Key operating forum	Grant-making (civil society) Tax (gvt)	Norm-making	Corporate-focused collaborating	Stakeholder-focused collaborating	Society-focused collaborating
Change type	First order, sometimes other	Second order	Second order	First or (usually) second order	Third, with second-order components

TABLE 5.3 Business motivations for sectoral engagement

The motivations take the names of common descriptions of business relation-ships with society, but these ordinary descriptions have a wide number of defini-tions and some people might not recognise those used here. In the same way as Table 4.1 described attributes of sectors in order to clarify the differences between the sectors, Table 5.3 aims to distinguish between motivations in order to have a more disciplined and thoughtful conversation about them and thereby develop more powerful strategies.

In this case philanthropy is thought of as 'giving' in its most altruistic form with anonymity and generosity. Affinity marketing and 'strategic' philanthropy that some associate with corporate philanthropy budgets are seen as mutual-gain strategies. Corporate social responsibility (CSR) and corporate citizenship (CC) are often used interchangeably. Here they are distinguished in particular by their 'relational system', which means the basis for corporations to form relationships with other sectors. In the case of CSR, the main driver is seen as a sense of 'obli-gation' in a *noblesse oblige* tradition defined by society's expectations—the 'norms' and the way corporations are expected to act. In this definition, the social respon-sibility movement is seen as trying to raise the standards of the norms.

Corporate citizenship, on the other hand, is envisioned as a framework based on rights and responsibilities *vis-à-vis* society at large. The corporation wants to

---

1 A report by the Center for Corporate Citizenship at Boston College has a different and also very helpful analysis with four motivations (CCC 2002).

renegotiate its rights and responsibilities. A classic example of this is with the corporations' drive to lengthen the time they hold patents, and the desire to reduce taxes or obtain corporate tax breaks. It is much more central to the core strategic concerns of the corporation than the CSR framework.

In this framework, the type of change is particularly important. Only SLC is third-order, deep change. The mutual gain and SLC frameworks are the most important because they are the most sustainable. Mutual gain is an exchange framework where one organisation does something in return for a collaborating organisation doing something. In the American banking example the bank changed its products and in return the community organisations facilitated promotion of the product; in the Canadian case the environmental organisations halted their promotion of a boycott of the forest companies' products and actually began promoting them in return for the company agreeing to a moratorium. In this mutual gain framework, negotiations and conflict resolution strategies are often important.

In the SLC motivation framework, however, development of a visionary collective strategy about how relationships can be changed fundamentally to favour the greater good is at play. In this motivation framework the interests of the corporation or other organisation are viewed as less important than the interests of greater humanity. This means that participants come with a willingness to rethink very basic rules of the game. The American bank developed a mutual-gain strategy in the context of an SLC mental model about the range of change.

Power is an important factor in all the frameworks. Only in the mutual-gain and SLC frameworks is power shared equitably—in the others there is an implicit assumption that the corporation will hold the most powerful position because the relationships come from a corporate-centric position where the well-being of the corporation is paramount. The depth of power-sharing in the SLC framework is much greater than in the mutual-gain one, however.

The point of this motivational framework is not that one is bad and that one is good, but that they can be mixed and leveraged to build an SLC initiative and to operationalise it. Different people, different parts of a business and different businesses will be more open to one type of motivation than another. An SLC relationship might begin with a philanthropic or mutual-gain connection, and as trust and mutual knowledge is built an SLC relationship can evolve. Certainly this is the history of the Canadian forestry case, which moved through several motivational frameworks—such as a philanthropic/mutual-gain one of giving up land for public use—before the SLC one emerged.

The CBO strategies

Unlike business, for CBOs societal change or provision of services and protection of communities are basic goals. Therefore, rather than analysing their roles in SLC initiatives in terms of motivations it is more useful to think of their actions from the point of view of strategy. Figure 5.1 suggests that there are four fundamental CBO strategies for engaging business based on two dimensions. The vertical *influence* dimension refers to how much the CBO is influenced by other sectors. This is thought of as its percentage of revenue provided by business or government (as opposed to donations or foundation funding) and the influence of those sectors on its board of directors. The *confrontation–collaboration* dimension refers to the degree that a CBO's interactions with another sector are through external processes such as advocacy and boycotts, or collaborative processes associated with deep dialogue and information-sharing. These four strategies are:

1. **Promoting change.** The CBO works from within civil society to influence other sectors rather than achieve third-order change. Examples include CBO-attached advisory boards made up of corporate members clearly under control of CBOs. For example, the neighbourhood coalition in the US banking case is a member of the National Community Reinvestment Coalition which has an advisory group of bankers. The core challenge in this strategy is to be relevant—often influence is very modest.

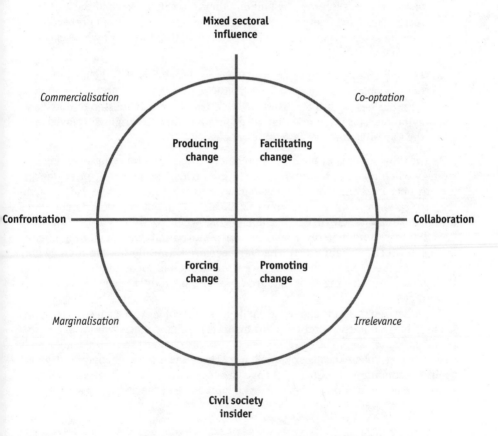

FIGURE 5.1 Four CBO strategies to influence other sectors

Source: Adapted from Waddell 2004

2. **Facilitating change.** CBOs intimately work with other sectors for mutual gain or SLC. Contracts between business and a CBO are often part of this strategy. Mvula Trust has this strategy working with other sectors in the South African water case. Here the big danger is co-optation—demonstrated by Mvula's concern about becoming a shareholder. This is also the strategy of TAI CBOs working with governments, and the GRI CBOs strategy working with business.

3. **Producing change.** CBOs often take on some core attributes of other sectors in order to infiltrate the sectors to either change them or provide alternatives. For example, in the Indian CTD case AWAKE is a women's small business incubator working with the CBO objective of furthering marginalised women's interests by building their capacity to work in the market sector. The danger here is commercialisation—AWAKE might simply become a business development consultant organisation and work for whoever can pay them.

4. **Forcing change.** CBOs often view the market sector itself as the major part of the problem, and in need of such basic reform that any CBO co-operation with business is suspect. These CBOs restrict their relationship to outside agitation. This is the role that the environmental CBOs originally played in the Canadian forestry case, for example.

As with the analysis of business motivations, there is not a right or wrong CBO strategy when it comes to working for SLC initiatives. The more advanced the SLC initiative becomes the more it tends to move into facilitating change. However, all the strategies have their potential role in an SLC initiative. At different times different strategies are needed and knowing when to shift is important. The Canadian case undoubtedly would not have moved into the facilitating change mode if the forcing change tactics had not been used. The appropriate strategy may differ with the type of initiative. Given the economic focus of the Indian and Philippines cases, having CBOs that are adept at the 'producing change' strategy is important.

The other key lesson is about the challenges that come with each strategy. Each strategy has a critical pitfall to guard against. Forcing change will fail if too few people are mobilised to be effective. For promoting change the critical challenge is to avoid irrelevance because of small size. Those facilitating change must guard against co-optation. 'Producing change' strategists must make sure they aggressively pursue innovation as the business adopts some of the greatest successes.

The role of government

Government has perhaps the most difficult role in SLC initiatives. This is because most often government comes with the mental model that it is supposed to be 'in charge'. Even when the word 'partnership' is used, for government this often means 'on our terms'. The implicit quality of the SLC world is that power is shared, everyone comes with their distinct powers and resources, and attempts to force decisions based on power will usually fail.

Government participates in SLC initiatives in order to meet its public obligations. Sometimes this means supporting the government to do this in a positive, proactive way, as with TAI CBOs building governments' capacity for participatory processes. But most often this means pushing government to take action, such as in the Canadian forestry case. Many times government actually takes leadership in developing the collaboration because it sees it as a way to fulfil its obligations. This is true in most of the remaining cases.

The government is facilitator of good process, creator of an 'enabling legislative environment' and a supporter of outcomes that benefit its citizens, rather than direct doer and implementer. The role of government in each case is worth looking at to understand its role in SLC initiatives more broadly:

- In the US banking case the federal government played an important role in creating an enabling environment by creating housing and small business programmes that are particularly well structured for bank–community partnerships. Perhaps most importantly it legislated the obligation of banks to have dialogues with communities and provide them information about their business and lending portfolios. The local government played an instrumental role in giving official status to the Community Development Advisory Committees, but only actively participated in times of crisis. The municipal government also mobilised other local public agencies to reward banks with good community lending practice with their business, and the threat of withdrawing it if the banks were to backslide.

- The government could be seen as initiating the Philippine SLC case through its land reform legislation. However, in most places land reform was not followed by successful restructuring as occurred in the case. The government provided legitimacy for the SLC initiative's development through its participation, and access to some modest resources such as high-quality seed and agriculture extension programmes.

- With the CTD in India, USAID and state government provided important convening and financial support for the initiative. Equally important was the activity of senior retired civil servants who knew how to work with government to access its programmes and resources as needed.

- The South African government has probably the most sophisticated public policy support for SLC, and actively encourages interaction between the three sectors in a number of ways. When a traditional for-profit consortium responded to its request for proposals to develop the water initiative, the government specifically directed it to team up with a proposal from the CBO Mvula Trust. It also provided funding and defined the objectives.

- The absence of direct government role in the Canadian forestry case is perhaps its most remarkable feature. The provincial government initially tried to resolve the issue on its own, but the other stakeholders rejected its solutions. Thereafter, the government's major role was to be supportive of the initiative as events warranted. For example, it facilitated job retraining and placement for unemployed loggers.

- The GRI is notable for the explicit absence of government. Bringing government into the initiative was seen by all as having a negative influence. Its presence would limit the experimental capacity of GRI since corporations would be less willing to innovate if they saw legislation impending. Rather, government is an outside observer of a process designed to raise standards and social norms to the point where government will be able to formalise the improvements in legislation.

- The government of Madagascar was notable in its willingness to transfer its authority over roads to the local road users' associations and to provide funding for their work.

- In TAI government has the most central role, since the SLC initiative focuses on changing government and building its capacity. Giving the TAI CBOs' facilitating change strategy, the government must be willing to change and learn how to improve its capacity for participatory decision-making in environmental issues.

Of course the bottom line in SLC initiatives is that participant organisations must be able to see clearly how participation will benefit them *and* be able to commit to a common vision and goals. The sense of 'benefit' must be grounded in a sense of the 'greater good' and supported by a sense that history is demanding change. The scale of change is often so great that participants exit quite different from how they entered. The Madagascar villagers entered as isolated farmers and exited in charge of their roads; the community groups in the US and Canadian cases entered as agitators and exited as collaborators; the companies in South Africa entered as construction and design firms and exited as suppliers of sustainable water systems.

References

CCC (Center for Corporate Citizenship) (2002) *Business and Community Development: Aligning Corporate Performance with Community Economic Development to Achieve Win-Win Impacts* (Boston, MA: Center for Corporate Citizenship).

Khan, A.H. (1997) 'The Orangi Pilot Project: Uplifting a Periurban Settlement near Karachi, Pakistan', in A. Krishna, N. Uphoff and M.J. Esman (eds.), *Reason for Hope* (West Hartford, CT: Kumarian Press): 29-40.

Plummer, J., and S. Waddell (2002) 'Building on the Assets of Potential Partners', in J. Plummer (ed.), *Focusing Partnerships: A Sourcebook for Municipal Capacity Building in Public–Private Partnerships* (London: Earthscan Publications).

Waddell, S. (2001) *What Works in Engaging Business in Youth Employment Strategies*. Vol. IV (Baltimore, MD: International Youth Foundation).

—— (2004) 'CBO Strategies to Engage Business: A Status Discussion Paper on Trends and Critical Issues' (Boston, MA: GAN-Net).

Chapter 6
What is the change process?

Thomas Kuhn popularised the concept of 'paradigm shift' in his famous book, *The Structure of Scientific Revolutions* (Kuhn 1962). This is the SLC scale of change that we need, to address the sustainability challenges facing us today. Kuhn investigated the processes physical sciences follow when they change the way they explain the world—such as the change from a earth-centric system to a heliocentric one to explain movements of the stars. The investigation revealed two essential processes that are equally relevant to SLC. One is amassing observations that cannot be explained by the traditional explanatory framework, and which thereby undermine its legitimacy. The second process is development of a new explanatory framework that can explain the new observations.

Kuhn's famous physical science deep change process and lesser-known ones from psychology, biology and sociology were compared in a famous article (Tushman and Romanelli 1985). These authors describe a process of large-scale change where contradictions, paradoxes and dilemmas become so numerous that traditional ways of doing things become untenable.

Broadly described, the contradictions, paradoxes and dilemmas behind the cases in this book can be summarised as the challenge of sustainability. That is to say that environmental, social, economic and political objectives are coming into such great conflict with each other that the prevailing rules of the game are breaking down. Environmental examples are perhaps the most obvious—traditional logging practices simply cannot continue because the forests are finite (Canadian forestry case), and traditional rules of the game for business cannot continue because environmental crises tell us they are unsustainable (GRI case).

However, contradictions with social outcomes are perhaps even stronger drivers in the cases. Although contemporary culture broadly speaking espouses basic human rights and equity, this contrasts with economic and political realities. The Canadian forestry case was also about equitable sharing of forest harvests with aboriginal and local communities; GRI is also about social equity for the marginalised and employees; the banking case is about fairness in the way banks operate.

Political contradictions are also obvious in the cases. For example, the Madagascar case was driven by the contradiction between the formal theory that the central government is responsible for roads and the fact that it could not meet its responsibilities; the Indian case by contradiction between the idea that government is responsible for economic development and the fact that it could not produce robust economic development on its own. In the South African case, the new approach resulted from failures in response to two theories—first, that government could provide water, and, second, that government and the private sector could do so together. And TAI (The Access Initiative) responded to the reality that international governmental agreements for most parts of the world are ineffective words on paper.

A common question is whether SLC is the product of crises or whether it can be a response to opportunity. Gersick writes about 'punctuated equilibrium' to describe a process where there is (1) equilibrium with one paradigm of explanatory and operating rules, (2) a period of contradictions with that paradigm amassing, and (3) a relatively quick transformation to a new paradigm and equilibrium (Gersick 1991). The cases suggest that during the period of contractions the SLC processes are a mixture of both crises and opportunity. Sometimes contradictions mount to the point of crisis and failure. At other times the contradictions lead to insights that are seen as opportunities, and change initiatives are initiated to develop them.

The Canadian forest, Madagascar road and American banking cases are the most classic examples of 'crises' with pitched battles, violence and personal desperation. In the other cases there were chronic but relatively low-level problems, and more of an opportunity-driven approach.

The change process consists of experiments with a small stakeholder community and continually expanding the change communities, based on successful experiments that attract more adherents and build an increasingly powerful new paradigm. For example, the Canadian forestry example began with one small inlet, one leading company and a subset of environmental CBOs. It expanded to a very large landmass of the Canadian west coast, the forest industry, aboriginal nations and many CBOs. Lessons from the Peddie community in South Africa were applied to other communities. The Indian economic development case is an example of continual expansion to engage new organisations by building on successes. TAI and GRI are global learning and capacity development communities where scaling-up is a critical task.

Organisational, network and societal development traditions provide a good framework for analysing in more detail the SLC process, and the cases provide ample information to illustrate it. In particular, work on development of public–private partnerships and intersectoral collaborations can be helpful (BPD 2001; Carson 2002; Fiszbein and Lowdin 1998; Gray 1989; Nelson 1996; Plummer and Waddell 2002; Tennyson and Wilde 2000; Waddell and Brown 1997). However, using for guidance *intra*-sectoral inter-organisational work with coalitions, joint ventures and alliances can cause problems since the core development challenges are very different.

SLC's distinctive features are very deep change and realignment of societal systems. The three orders of change introduced in Chapter 1 are shown in Figure 6.1. Although first- and second-order change will inevitably be part of SLC initiatives, these will occur against a background of third-order change. Through dialogue and exchange of information participants in SLC initiatives challenge one another's stereotypes and assumptions in order to explore how they can work together differently. For example, in the Madagascar case the assumption that villagers were incapable of maintaining their own roads and that the central government had to provide them was challenged. As in the Madagascar case, SLC challenges often mean that new skills and organisations need to be built—the second- and first-order changes. However, these follow changes in beliefs and assumptions. The Madagascar villagers had to be trained in road maintenance and running their road users' associations, but first the assumptions had to be uncovered and tested.

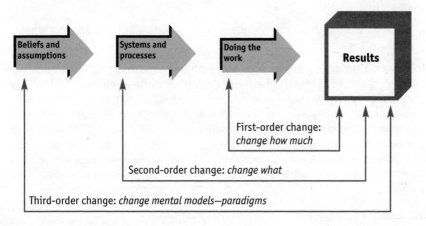

FIGURE 6.1 Three orders of change

Source: David Stroh, Bridgeway Partners, 2003

The change processes can be divided into stages. These can be cut and sliced in many ways, but they provide a sequence of activities that can be easily adapted to specific situations. In this case we break the process into three stages: preparing the ground, achieving the goals and building capacity for greater results. These are broken down into a total of six consecutive steps. Each of these steps can be best explained by introducing some questions that must be answered before moving on.

Of course these steps should be treated as a good guide rather than strict rules. Steps merge into one another, and sometimes idiosyncratic qualities and opportunities demand some shifting. However, moving on to another step should only be done after assessing if it really is time to do so.

Stage one: preparing the ground

This is the stage where you analyse the situation and learn more about what is involved in an SLC initiative. Traditional research into the issue and opportunity is called for. By the end of this stage you will be ready for a meeting.

Step 1: Learning about SLCs—building your own understanding

1. Why develop an SLC?
2. What are 'organisational sectors'?

3. What are the potential benefits of an SLC approach over intra-organisational and intra-sectoral activities?

4. In what types of situations are SLC initiatives appropriate?

5. How are SLC initiatives different from partnerships in a single organisation or sector?

6. What is an SLC development process, how long does it take and what resources are needed?

Most people involved in starting SLC initiatives have substantive technical knowledge in the key issue of the 'problem/opportunity' such as road-building, environmental sciences, youth employment, economics, infrastructure construction, standards development, marketing or new product development. However, organisational, network and societal learning and development skills and knowledge provide the backbone for SLC strategies. Therefore, people considering SLC initiatives can best start by learning about SLC, how to assess whether it represents an appropriate strategy and, if so, how to support their development.

Step 2: Identifying the options—researching opportunities

1. What is a common definition of the nature of the problem/opportunity?

2. What is the problem/opportunity and who does it affect?

3. How are key stakeholder groups affected by the problem?

4. To what extent are resources from different stakeholders required?

5. What is the history of the issue?

6. What are the stakeholders' organisational capacities for an SLC initiative?

7. What are the key organisations and players in the sectors?

8. Are key stakeholders 'ready' for collaboration? What are the impediments?

9. What present or potential coalitions exist among key actors?

10. To what extent is the issue widely perceived as a 'crisis', so otherwise reluctant parties might be willing to try something new?

11. What is the organisational capacity of the stakeholders to work together?

SLC initiatives involve significant resources, so it makes sense to take the time to learn about the options, analyse the opportunities and determine whether the potential is worth the effort. Most individuals and organisations have no systematic way of thinking about the benefits of collaboration among sectors, or lack the skills to realise them. Most organisations simply do not collaborate enough with organisations in other sectors to learn about one another, explore how they might work together, overcome stereotypes and build trust.

This analysis must take a systems perspective where stakeholders are defined *vis-à-vis* an issue rather than an organisation. Sliding into a perspective where stakeholders are thought of *vis-à-vis* a particular organisation will lead to failure since people are unlikely to want to focus on an organisation's success as opposed to successfully addressing an issue or opportunity of common interest.

A situation analysis includes assessing the potential benefits of collaboration with regard to a specific industry, group, issue or geography. Have other approaches been attempted and failed? The tables presented earlier on core competences and attributes help sharpen this analysis and develop a firmer rationale for the collaboration (Table 4.1).

'Mapping' the key stakeholders and their relationships to define 'the system' is very useful. This should include analysing current capacity to realise the multi-sector potential based on institutions, attitudes, policies, leadership and skills. Such analysis requires interviewing people and learning about their relationships with other people to develop a social networks map (Allee 2003; Cross and Parker 2004; Krebs and Holley 2004). Often there are people and organisations that do not immediately surface as the 'leaders' and opinion-influencers, so this work must be done carefully. A disciplined data-gathering research process that builds a database is recommended; in large initiatives network mapping software can prove invaluable.

One example of mapping done with GRI in South Africa is given in Figure 6.2. This was developed to help GRI organise more effectively in South Africa. It involved a series of interviews with people working on GRI-associated issues about their inter-organisational relationships. It revealed five important sub-networks with key bridging organisations indicated by the diamonds. The interviews did not reveal any bridges to one network—that of environmentalists.[1] This type of analysis derives from the perspective that SLC initiatives should arise from *current* social relationships rather than building something brand-new. This vastly speeds trust-building and supports building a strategy where the social ties are knit together from distinct networks in a comprehensive way.

The Indian, Madagascar, South African, GRI and TAI cases went through quite extensive research processes, although we now know how to do this better, based on our SLC learning and tools such as network mapping. The banking and forestry cases grew out of crises and therefore the research developed in a more haphazard and chaotic way. The Philippine case depended on the research leadership of a particularly credible individual.

Stage two: achieving the goals

Now you are ready to bring people together, and have people jointly identify where they want to go and their roles in getting there. At this point the work should move into a participatory action learning/action research mode. This means summarising the leading knowledge about how to address the issue organisationally and creating a disciplined process with the stakeholders to try out possible solutions in a learning environment (Reason and Bradbury 2000; Selener 1997).

---

1   A more thorough analysis would probably have revealed such an organisation. However, other data confirmed that the environmental bottom line is the weakest in South Africa.

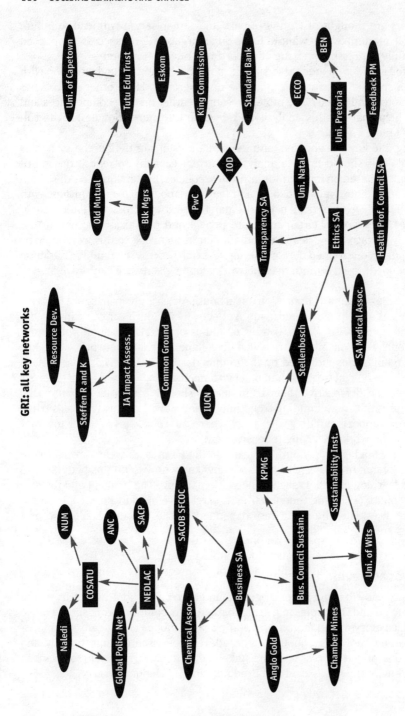

FIGURE 6.2 Mapping of South African social network

Source: Waddell and Allee 2002

Step 3: Getting the idea off the ground—cultivating the stakeholders

1. How should the sectoral representatives be brought together?
2. What is the purpose of the meeting?
3. Who should call the meeting?
4. Where should the meeting be held?
5. What rules should govern the meeting?
6. How can the parties establish a climate of optimism and a willingness to try new alternatives, especially when there is often a context of conflict or blame?
7. What processes can be used to explore differences and common interests?
8. How can the parties reach a joint definition of the issue?
9. What are the ingredients of a successful definition?

If analysis shows that an SLC strategy makes sense, the research provides data to clearly identify which parties should be brought together to explore opportunities and how the exploration should occur. The basic concept is to bring together all the key stakeholders who make up 'the system'—all the organisations that influence or are influenced by the focal issue or opportunity. Sometimes these will only be representatives from the key components identified in the previous research, rather than *all* the organisations. For example, in the Philippines three organisations that collectively represented all the components of an envisioned new rice production system were brought together. And sometimes the goal is closer to bringing together all of the potential stakeholders. This was the case in India when the case first started and a broad invitation to participate was issued. Remember that at times the needed organisations do not even exist, and their construction is a key task to be integrated into development. This was the case with the road users' associations in Madagascar, for example.

This stage deals with construction of a 'container' for the SLC. All the participants will have to go through the same analytical process that the initiator went through in Steps 1 and 2. Workshops play an important role, but they must be devised with reference to the issue that is inspiring people to work together. The convening process should develop trust at this stage to build successfully through other stages. Power differences and issues of insider/outsider must be addressed. Potential benefits and roles for the participants should be identified.

Often it is best to first gather organisations from the three sectors separately, for them to discuss the issue among themselves, clarify their objectives and identify concerns. In the Canadian forestry example, it was critical that the CBOs and businesses had their own places to discuss their strategies before coming together. Tables 4.2. 4.3 and 4.4 on core competences can be very helpful in leading the discussion in a constructive way. In addition, getting the groups to talk about the issue and picture it in terms of a whole system with all the stakeholders helps strengthen understanding of the need for collaboration. They can develop maps, such as the one presented from South Africa, based on their own experience.

Step 4: Defining the plans—optimising outcomes for all

1. How can stakeholders develop plans that respect their different strengths and interests?

2. What are the goals of each participating organisation?

3. Who will provide resources?

4. Is there enough mutual commitment of key stakeholders to move ahead?

5. Who will provide the necessary resources?

6. How can different perspectives be combined to develop strategies that make good use of their diverse resources?

7. How can further exploration, work and planning develop interactively?

At Step 4 the stakeholders come together for the first time. It is useful to think of this as a 'large system intervention', where the purpose is to bring greater coherence and realise the latent potential of currently unconnected efforts (Holman and Devane 1999). The goal is not to manage or co-ordinate in any strict sense but to create interactions between system participants so that they can discover ways to work together to more effectively achieve their distinct goals.

Sometimes one organisation (such as a foundation) or person who is perceived by all as a trusted party creates and financially supports a key initiating event. USAID and the government of the state of Karnataka were co-hosts for the India case, and there was a similar arrangement in Madagascar. In the South African case, the relationships grew out of an RfP (request for proposals) where the government stipulated that the business group team up with Mvula Trust. Sometimes the initiative grows out of existing relationships. For example, GRI grew out of relationships that business and CBOs had in the organisation CERES. In the Philippine and US banking cases, an individual respected by all the stakeholders was critical. The Canadian forestry cases grew out of conflict and the forest company's Linda Coady became a particularly trusted interlocutor.

Numerous large system planning processes are possible, but most require an intense period together—usually two and a half days is considered critical because of the way people integrate their experiences through sleep and to achieve the necessary amount of work. The outcome should be some relatively clear plans for what each participant is going to do next. Some intersectoral groups should be established. Although one group might have an administrative function, the formation of project groups is particularly important.

Step 5: Implementing the plans—getting the results

1. How can the plans be successfully implemented?

2. How can the inevitable tensions and conflicts that arise among actors be addressed?

3. How will decisions be handled, and to what extent is participation by grass-roots groups required?

4. What kinds of capacity-building are necessary for different actors to play their parts?

Simply going through a joint planning and visioning process is an important achievement. However, this is only the beginning of realising the desired outcomes, and other problems will arise along the way. Steps can be taken to overcome lethargy in relationships, address crises and adapt successes to new locations or issues.

Keeping the relationships work-based and focused is key in avoiding unproductive theoretical discussion which can quickly lead to participants drifting away. The work should be hitched to a reasonable time goal, and an outside imperative beyond the collaboration's direct control can be particularly powerful. One reason TAI was so successful is that it was committed to producing a methodology for the World Summit on Sustainable Development in Johannesburg in 2002. However, more often the goals are set internally.

Successful collaborations are based on clearly articulated outcomes for all participants, as well as for the collaboration as a whole. The outcomes must be clear enough and sufficiently achievable that all participants will be committed to each other's success. Amanz'abantu in South Africa was plagued by inadequate goal definition *in terms of the distinct goals of the partners*—although they had clear collective goals. This both led to confusing friction, and meant there was no process or framework to investigate some endemic dissatisfaction. With clearly set goals at the beginning (often framed in terms of 'ranges') and an evaluation process, collaboration members have a better way to assess success or what is possible, and to know what failure means.

One common problem is that in SLC initiatives people can unconstructively 'blame' others for problems. To avoid this, it is useful to treat SLC initiatives as learning and capacity-building processes. This requires well-defined learning activities that parallel the 'real work' to create a supportive operating environment and minimise problems by quickly addressing them as they arise.

A learning strategy is particularly important for SLC initiatives given that so many of them deal with many complex and innovative approaches. One source of GRI's success was that it identified what it did not know, and set up a process to bring people with leading knowledge related to both the measurement construction and organising questions of GRI, before deciding what made sense for GRI. This integration of research and action is highly superior to the classic consultant-based approach of taking a narrow range of experience that may be weakly relevant to the key SLC initiative, and taking action based on that.

When conflict arises, assessing it in terms of the type of change it is associated with is helpful. For example, with first- and second-order change a negotiations approach to conflict resolution is often useful. However, sometimes when the problem concerns second-order change and always when it concerns third-order change, traditional conflict resolution and negotiations strategies can actually be detrimental. They are not good at handling transformative change. For example, in the Philippine case a question of profit allocation versus capital investment in the CBO and business joint enterprise is essentially a first-order change—it does not threaten to disrupt the balance of the relationship but simply reallocates joint resources. However, a shift in profit allocation between the two partners is a second-order change and more sensitive since it implies a shift in perception of the costs one partner is incurring or the benefits it should be receiving. But most complicated is when one of the basic underpinnings of the relationship comes up for consideration. For example, for the Philippine farmers environmentally friendly farming practices were critical. If they wanted to extend that goal to the operations of Dolefil itself as a condition of continuing, a much different resolution strategy would be necessary since the entire relationship would be at risk. This type of third-order change requires much deeper re-visioning processes.

Stage three: building capacity for greater results

Step 6: Continuing the development cycle—scaling up, terminating and sharing lessons

1. What is the appropriate process for expanding the activity?

2. How can lethargy be overcome?

3. When and how should an SLC initiative be terminated?

As for all organisations, the question of growth and death are part of the SLC development cycle. Given that SLC initiatives require substantial effort and invest-ment, and given that they produce important social capital and trust as the basis for working together more, a drive for growth makes sense.

Expansion and replication of success requires identification of strategies that customise key learning and recognise inhibiting factors. This involves compiling lessons and a new round of planning, often with historic partners supporting the development of new ones.

However, the business growth strategies grounded in issues of ownership, equity and managerial control provide very poor guidance for SLC expansion. There are two basic reasons. One is that those strategies do not account for the voluntary nature that is a core element of SLC initiatives—you cannot 'buy' or 'merge owner-ship' of an SLC initiative. Second, business growth is accompanied by a degree of standardisation and control that make impossible the participatory processes and responsiveness to local circumstances that are essential to SLC initiatives' success. Consequently, the 'rolling-out' of new products and franchising strategies of business simply will not work with SLC initiatives.

A much more useful growth concept comes from CBOs and civil society. This is the concept of 'scaling-up', which means to increase impact and build on knowledge and skills rather than becoming large. One study (Uvin *et al.* 2000) identified four ways that CBOs do this:

1. **Expanding coverage and size.** This quantitative scaling-up is the closest to the business model, and means building on a successful base by setting up more offices and sub-networks. This is most obviously part of the TAI global process. TAI is expanding the number of countries where it is opera-

tional. In the Canadian forestry case this occurred as the participants shifted their attention from the original Clayoquot Sound to the entire coast of British Columbia.

2. **Increasing activities to expand the products.** This functional scaling-up means moving from one activity to include another. This is perhaps the most difficult type of scaling-up for an SLC initiative, since the original activities represent a careful and intricate weaving-together of interests. It is difficult to find additional activities that can be based on the original participants, and this type of expansion is likely to be dangerous. This is one reason that GRI has been so reluctant to move beyond creation of a reporting framework to more actively supporting implementation of the framework. However, the banking SLC case might be viewed through this expansion strategy, as it has continually expanded the number of products and services developed through the intersectoral forum.

3. **Broadening indirect impact.** Indirect activities are ones that seek to influence the behaviour of others. This is perhaps the most important scaling-up strategy for SLC initiatives, and occurs in two ways. One is through replication, with another group replicating or adapting an SLC strategy to its own situation. This is the way the Madagascar road user case is being expanded: an increasing number of communities are taking the idea and applying it. However, the impact may be even more indirect. TAI hopes to expand the impact of its drive to transformation, by changing government's behaviour not just with respect to itself but also through its regulatory practice with respect to the private sector as well. This strategy raises critical questions about the tipping point—how much the SLC innovation has to expand before it is widely adopted or alters the concept of what is standard practice (Gladwell 2002).

    In the forestry case the tipping point seems to have been reached with respect to the shift from traditional clear-cut logging practices; the banking case has generally been poorly imitated in the banking sector, as simple public relations exercises, but some banks have also adopted similar core business strategies; GRI is driving to increase the number of companies using its framework in the belief that this is a critical tipping-point strategy.

4. **Enhancing organisational sustainability.** This means increasing in size based on the need to be sustainable and taking account of lessons learned with SLC initiatives. It is often associated with the shift from a pilot project to large-scale application. The most direct and simplistic example of this is with expansion in the Philippines from an initial experiment with a few farmers to a viable commercial operation.

    However, for SLC initiatives this particular scaling-up strategy takes an unusual twist since an SLC initiative is a pilot for all of its participants to use elsewhere. One exciting aspect of SLC initiatives is that they include a diverse number of participants that in turn possess broad and diverse networks for dissemination of lessons and scaling-up through enhancing organisational sustainability. For example, the large companies involved in the South African water and sanitation case are taking the lessons learned there and applying them to their operations elsewhere in the world. For the UN, both GRI and TAI have been influential in the way it thinks of global governance and the model has led to strong support for similar (Type II) arrangements.

The exciting innovative aspect of SLC initiatives is driven by the participants' different resources and perspectives. However, after a while a fatigue develops in an SLC collaboration. This might signal that the partners have become so comfortable with one another that they have actually lost their distinctive logics and become much like each other. Participants may no longer challenge one another about their assumptions or achieving a common good, since one or the other has become dominant. This means the very rationale for the collaboration has disappeared. One way to address this is to do an audit against the attributes table presented in Chapter 4, to see how the partners have changed and to try to re-spark the original differences.

However, lethargy can also indicate that the collaboration has simply fallen into performing a valued and routine function. Or, sometimes it means that the collaboration should be wound up since its goals have been achieved. One SLC initiative, the World Commission on Dams, was set up with a pre-set duration and a narrowly defined task around identifying strategies that would integrate business, civil society and government concerns about large dam projects. However, an important implementation task followed its report. This task was transferred to a UN agency where it lost its distinctive energy and became marginalised.

Stories describing successes, failures, problems and they way they were addressed inspire others; they may celebrate achievements and provide important guiding lessons that can be adapted to many locations. This can be integrated into the learning strategy, with collaborators writing their history and, throughout the process, raising issues that need to be addressed. Sometimes comparative analysis with similar collaborations or the creating of joint learning communities helps spur collaborations in new directions. This is particularly important for network SLC initiatives such as TAI and GRI. Documentation is a valued process for sharing stories with others who are going through their own collaboration development, and for building collaboration skills more widely. After all, these skills are a key part of constructing a better world.

Six classic mistakes

There are six classic mistakes that are made in SLC initiatives. 'Mistakes' are approaches that make the entire development process more costly, risky and longer than need be. These can easily sink an initiative, particularly considering that the cases demonstrate that a minimum of three and usually more years are necessary before an SLC initiative begins achieving the scale of impact that was originally envisioned.

One classic mistake is *jumping in without having done the necessary groundwork.* People like to be action-oriented and often find it hard to follow a disciplined development process. For many people, calling a meeting with some people who you think of as stakeholders in the issue to talk about what can be done together seems an obvious first step. Only later do the problems that this approach can cause become obvious. Bringing the wrong group of people together might quickly result in issues about expansion or exclusion. Good preparation can avoid bringing together people who are incapable of working together or even of having effective conversations. And sometimes, such as with the Madagascar villagers, the capacity of a stakeholder group to work together must first be built before an intersectoral meeting.

A second mistake, related to the first, is being *event-focused rather than process-focused.* People often decide the dates for one or two major meetings, announce them publicly and then start to discuss in detail what is necessary to make the meetings successful. Only then do they start to realise the meeting dates are wrong and effort becomes focused on making the meetings successful rather than the development process successful. And sometimes people just do not consider important tangential factors. For example, in one case another major international event that was going to require substantial effort from the same group of stakeholders who were being targeted for the SLC initiative was not taken into account. Both of these problems arose with GRI organising in South Africa.

The third classic mistake is *underestimating the distinctive intersectoral qualities* of an SLC initiative and making inappropriate comparisons with other experiences. In particular, people think of SLC initiatives as 'inter-organisational' and fail to account for the 'intersectoral' qualities—business people draw inappropriate experience from business joint ventures, CBO people from civil society coalitions and government officials from inter-governmental processes. Consultants who have only worked in one sector can be particularly problematic, since they will provide advice without even understanding the number of assumptions that their advice is based on. People presume 'we all want the same thing' and that organisational logics are the same; they even fail to recognise that words used in one sector can mean very different things in other sectors. These were pernicious problems in the South African water example, as the different operating frames of administering, managing and developing continually clashed.

The fourth classic mistake is *underestimating the distinctive third-order change qualities* of an SLC initiative and making inappropriate comparisons with other experiences. Often people apply first- and second-order change strategies to develop SLC initiatives. They use negotiations and conflict resolution strategies, rather than visioning and inspirational strategies. The former can be useful in later stages, but if they are used in the early stages people probably will never be able to develop the creative space necessary for SLC. This proved a hindrance in the Indian economic development case. Rather than developing ongoing forums where diverse groups could get together, the leaders of the initiative saw themselves more as brokers between the various interests. This meant that CBOs in particular were marginalised in the process, since the leaders' relationships with them were weak.

A fifth classic mistake is *failing to understand that repetitive cycles of development are necessary and take time.* Usually an SLC initiative begins as an insight of one or two people after they investigate a situation. Then a larger core group will be convened that will have to go through the same learning process; and very often another expansion in membership will occur which again will require repeating the process. This requires a conscious process of continually rebuilding the SLC 'container' or sponsorship group.

A sixth classic mistake is *thinking that you should define your organisational structure, relationship and decision-making processes and then do the work*. This is a guarantee for wasting time in talking about things that are not important, creating a structure that will actually inhibit your ability to be effective, and cause people to drift away. The well-known rule is that 'structure follows strategy', and to get a strategy you have to have some experience. Begin by actually undertaking activity to address the issue, and draw lessons about what works from your experience. TAI spent two years with partners in nine locations working together on a trial basis before focusing on the organisational structure; the GRI spent five years.

References

Allee, V. (2003) *The Future of Knowledge: Increasing Prosperity through Value Networks* (New York: Butterworth-Heinemann).

BPD (Business Partners for Development) (2001) *Enduring Myths, Enduring Truths: Enabling Partnerships between Business, Civil Society and the Public Sector* (Washington, DC: World Bank).

Carson, A.S. (2002) 'Establishing Public–Private Partnerships: Three Tests of a Good Process', *International Applied Business Research Conference*, Puerto Vallarta, Mexico.

Cross, R., and A. Parker (2004) *The Hidden Power of Social Networks* (Boston, MA: Harvard Business School).

David Strohe, Bridgeway Partners (2003) personal paper (Lexington, MA).

Fiszbein, A., and P. Lowdin (1998) *Working Together for a Change: Government, Business and Civic Partnerships for Poverty Reduction in LAC* (Washington, DC: World Bank).

Gersick, C. (1991) 'Revolutionary Change Theories: A Multilevel Exploration of the Punctuated Equilibrium Paradigm', *Academy of Management Review* 16: 10-36.

Gladwell, M. (2002) *The Tipping Point: How Little Things Can Make a Big Difference* (Boston, MA: Little, Brown & Company).

Gray, B.G. (1989) *Collaborating: Finding Common Ground for Multiparty Problems* (San Francisco: Jossey-Bass).

Holman, P., and T. Devane (1999) *The Change Handbook: Group Methods for Shaping the Future* (San Francisco: Berrett-Koehler).

Krebs, V., and J. Holley (2004) 'Building Sustainable Communities through Social Network Development', *The Non-Profit Quarterly* 10: 40-53.

Kuhn, T. (1962) *The Structure of Scientific Revolutions* (Chicago: University of Chicago Press).

Nelson, J. (1996) *Business as Partners in Development: Creating Wealth for Countries, Companies and Communities* (London: Prince of Wales Business Leaders Forum in collaboration with the World Bank and the United Nations Development Programme).

Plummer, J., and S. Waddell (2002) 'Building on the Assets of Potential Partners', in J. Plummer (ed.), *Focusing Partnerships: A Sourcebook for Municipal Capacity Building in Public–Private Partnerships* (London: Earthscan Publications).

Reason, P., and H. Bradbury (2000) *The Handbook of Action Research* (Newbury Park, CA: Sage Publications).

Selener, D. (1997) *Participatory Action Research and Social Change* (Ithaca, NY: Cornell Participatory Action Research Network).

Tennyson, R., and L. Wilde (2000) *The Guiding Hand: Brokering Partnerships for Sustainable Development* (New York: United Nations Department of Public Information).

Tushman, M.L., and E. Romanelli (1985) 'Organizational Evolution: A Metamorphosis Model of Convergence and Reorientation', in L.L. Cummings and B.M. Staw (eds.), *Research in Organizational Behavior.* Vol. VI (Greenwich, CT: JAI Press).

Uvin, P., P. Jain and L.D. Brown (2000) *Scaling Up NGO Programs in India: Strategies and Debates.* Vol. XVI (Boston, MA: Institute for Development Research, www.jsi.com/idr).

Waddell, S., and V. Allee (2002) *GRI Network Development: South Africa* (Boston, MA: GAN-Net)

—— and L.D. Brown (1997) *Fostering Intersectoral Partnering: A Guide to Promoting Cooperation Among Government, Business, and Civil Society Actors.* Vol. XIII (Boston, MA: Institute for Development Research).

Chapter 7
What are the SLC structures?

Societal learning and change is a new way for people, organisations and sectors to relate to one another. The bankers and community development activists, the forest companies and environmental CBOs, the national governments and TAI CBOs, the corporations and GRI CBOs had to move from relationships of antagonism to mutuality. The Madagascar and Indian governments had to shift from thinking of themselves as 'in control' to playing a supportive role. The construction companies in South Africa and Dolefil in the Philippines had to shift from thinking of themselves as independent producers to being part of a bigger interdependent system. These new types of relationships cannot be built on old types of structures. SLC requires new ways of organising.

Elements of this new form of organising are found under many labels: collaborative enterprise (Halal 2001); social partnerships (Waddock 1989, 1991); strategic alliances (Austin 1998); collaborative alliances (Gray and Wood 1991); public–private partnerships (Carson 2002); government–business–civic partnerships; tri-sector partnerships (Perlas 2000; Warner 2000; NRC–BPD 2001); and catalytic alliances (Waddock and Post 1995). The distinctive element of SLC is the depth of change. While many partnerships involve relatively minor change (first and second order), SLC initiatives involve fundamental change. They are *not* merely contractual, although contracts are often a tool. They are a new way of putting together the emotional, mental and physical core distinctions of the three sectors, which is reflected by a new way of organising.

The critical shift is from a mental model in which the emotional, mental and physical should be separated or in which one should be dominant, to a mental model where they are working together in an integrated manner. This does *not* mean that the distinctions are simply merged together in a type of oneness, but that they learn to dance and weave together to create a more harmonious whole while maintaining their identities. In this book the word 'collaboration' is used as distinct from 'partnership'. The former is seen as different logics working together (inter-sectoral and inter-organisational), whereas the latter is seen as same logics working together (intra-sectoral and intra-organisational such as business-to-business).

Using the title of 'issue management alliances', Austrom and Lad described a shift in the logics that is represented by the alliances and by SLC (Table 7.1).

> The prevailing paradigm of industrial society is based on a mechanistic model of the universe which had its genesis in the mathematical formula-

PREVAILING PARADIGM	EMERGENT PARADIGM
Basic world-view	
● Mechanistic ● Cartesian	● Holistic, open systems ● Ecological
Implicit logics	
● Focus on distinctions and separations ● Either–or oppositions ● Dualities as opposites and contradictions	● Focus on interdependence and interrelatedness ● Both–and relations ● Dualities as paradoxes
Leading values	
● Self-contained individualism and agency ● Zero-sum game mentality ● Win–lose orientation	● Communitarianism and communion ● Positive-sum game mentality ● Win–win orientation

TABLE 7.1 The new logics

Source: Austrom and Lad 1989

tions of Descartes and Newton. This has resulted in design principles of organisations as 'centralised, large scale, bureaucratic and hierarchical' (Austrom and Lad 1989).

The new paradigm is referred to as 'ecological and holistic', a description together with 'biology' that has been repeated many times when referring to a new organising principle (see, for example, Wheatley 1992; Maturana and Varela 1998). In accord with the new logic of both–and, the emergent paradigm will not replace the prevailing one but will become the dominant one due to the crises (such as environmental) and values (such as for greater equity) that cannot be addressed by the traditional paradigm.

The new paradigm of Austrom and Lad and the eight cases generate the key organisational design principles for creating SLC initiatives. These include interdependence, subsidiarity, mutual accountability and effectiveness.

Designing for interdependence

SLC initiatives are forums for stakeholder interactions. These are not stakeholders in an organisation, but in an issue. They need not be *all* stakeholders in an issue— but for success there must be sufficient power to address the issue and no stakeholders who can block the issue can be in active opposition.

This interdependence and issue stakeholder perspective means that paying attention to the place where the stakeholders meet is not sufficient for success. The relationships between that meeting place and the participants in the SLC initiative also must be understood. Thinking of the stakeholder relationships as production systems of collaborating organisations, these can be labelled as 'full-system co-production' structures (Waddell 2002). In this analysis the production is a public good and a reframed private good. Examples are:

- Sustainable forestry (public) and sustainable forestry wood products (private)

- Community development, and new bank products and delivery strategies

- Economic development using public university knowledge, and new businesses and strengthened industries

- Roads and security, and access to markets

The traditional idea of a 'production chain' with a series of activities linearly linked does not fit with the SLC model (Waddell 2000). Rather, there is a more complex set of relationships, as a system perspective would suggest. Mapping the relationships between the stakeholders in the cases reveals three basic types of structure.

Forward capacity-building SLC initiatives

This full-system co-production approach is particularly complicated and is represented by the GRI and TAI cases. There are at least two customers: the company or government involved is itself a client, and then there are the end-consumers (citizens for government; customers for businesses) of the products. These SLC initiatives help a business or government get its work done in a more sustainable process by connecting to CBOs' community networks and core competences. The variety of businesses and governments involved in these cases suggests that this SLC type is applicable in a variety of industries and government levels.

The capacity-building SLC is well illustrated with GRI (see Fig. 7.1). For business, GRI is an important supplier of CBO skills and knowledge about how to address environmental problems and work with communities. It also supplies business with trust that the civil society organisations have with communities and workers. For example, in South Africa, GRI is developing a broad-based approach to address HIV/AIDS as a workplace and community issue. This illustrates the way business acts both as supplier—the approach would be impossible without businesses' involvement—and as client since it is itself receiving a solution to a business problem (a uniform standard, community accountability structure). As is typical with capacity-building SLC initiatives, these activities respond to a relatively amorphous system concern (sustainability), rather than a particular group of customers.

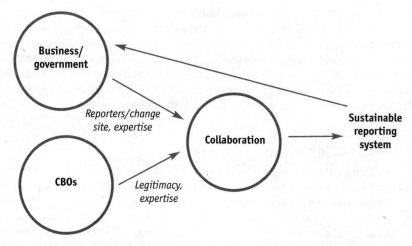

FIGURE 7.1 Capacity-building SLC: GRI

Back-end SLC initiatives

The Canadian forestry, Philippine rice and Indian economic development cases are examples of this type of SLC (see Fig. 7.2). These SLC initiatives have a traditional relationship with end-use customers who receive their goods via traditional delivery channels, and may be entirely unaware of the negative social and environmental externalities behind their production.

This type of SLC appears to occur in the natural resource sector, including agriculture. Business provides consumers with access to more sustainable products, and

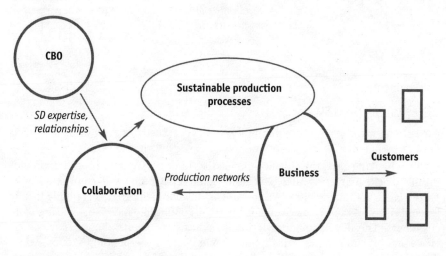

FIGURE 7.2 Back-end SLC

CBOs organise their communities into sizable units, provide technical expertise, and are stewards for the sustainability agenda. For example, in the Philippines, the CBO organised the farmer-producers into a large enough production unit to produce the volume that Dolefil needs. It provides technical expertise on organic farming and represents the farmers in negotiations around price and other arrangements. The government provides important support through the Department of Agriculture's education programmes and the provision of high-quality rice seed.

Front-end SLC initiatives

The US banking, the South African water and the Madagascar road-building cases are examples of front-end SLC initiatives (see Fig. 7.3). In this SLC, the end-customer —or at least customer representatives—actually becomes involved in the definition and delivery of the product. The representatives are in the form of CBOs, usually led by members of the community purchasing the product. The CBO also often plays an important role of market/community organising to make it of sufficient scale that the business can justify undertaking its work in this way. Construction and provision of infrastructure (including financial infrastructure) dominate this type of SLC.

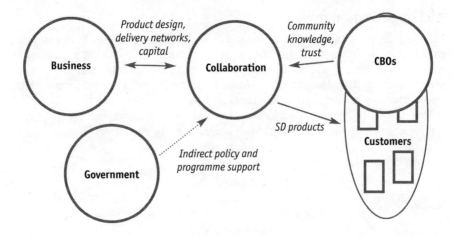

FIGURE 7.3 Front-end SLC

In the banking case, the collaboration assists in designing new products, providing feedback, marketing and education, loan repayment, and co-ordination of participants' complementary initiatives. The development groups are truly locally led and run, and their role is well known to the community members who are bank customers. The development group helps educate residents about financial services, and provides them with support (sometimes as peer lending groups) when repayment of loans becomes a problem. This support is dramatically less expensive than traditional legal processes for enforcing loan repayment. The government plays important support roles both locally through its purchasing power, which favours banks involved in such work, and at the federal level through regulations and programme support for activities such as low-income housing.

Designing for subsidiarity and autonomy

This second design principle may seem contradictory to the first. However, the SLC initiatives address their issues through solutions that optimise the engagement of those closest to the issue, while maintaining independence among the participating organisations. As Chapter 4 explained, the basic rationale for SLC initiatives is to access the distinct sectoral resources and strengths, and offset their weaknesses. This is the driving collective reasoning behind increasing organisational interdependence, and if organisations become too mutually dependent and alike they will lose the distinctive qualities that were the rationale for bringing them together in the first place.

Subsidiarity describes the principle that a higher authority should only intervene in the work of a lower authority to the extent necessary to achieve a specific purpose. The Council of Europe defined subsidiarity as 'endeavour(ing) as far as possible to manage affairs as closely to the citizen as possible and to depart from this principle only for reasons of absolute necessity' (Council of Europe 1994). Sometimes the lower authority (i.e. citizen) has demonstrated incapacity and therefore needs help. Sometimes the lower authority is acting in a way that has negative impact on others, so that a higher authority must intervene. Much SLC action is driven by Albert Einstein's insight that solutions to a problem cannot be resolved at the level at which they have been created. Therefore, the SLC structure is created with different levels that can respond to a problem in order to influence other levels.

The autonomy principle means that participants in a collaboration aim only to influence one another to the extent necessary to address the focal issue. The collaboration forum is a separate space from the participants' organisations, and is guided by distinct rules. This means, for example, that the participants abide by a set of principles that they agree to with respect to their own interactions, but that the participants do not hold one another to those principles with respect to interactions beyond the scope of the collaboration—unless this is agreed to. This distinction is part of the essence of a *chaordic* organisation (Hock 1999).

The reason for this is simple. Organisations participating in SLC initiatives are often large and complex, and an SLC initiative only forms a small part of their overall activity. Yet the SLC initiative involves fundamental change. As anyone involved in change processes knows, changing all at once is impossible. While there is a reasonable expectation that with time and success the principles of the SLC and its strategies will impact more widely through its participants' behaviour, such a commitment cannot be made upfront. Moreover, the principles guiding the SLC to success are not necessarily the ones that will guide the participants' success with other tasks.

Chaordic is a word invented by Dee Hock and comes from combining CHAos and ORDer. 1: Any autocatalytic, self-regulating, adaptive, non-linear, complex organism, organisation or system, whether physical, biological or social, the behaviour of which harmoniously exhibits characteristics of both order and chaos. 2: An entity whose behaviour exhibits patterns and probabilities not governed or explained by the behaviour of its parts. 3: The fundamental organising principle of nature and evolution. See www.chaord.org.

Box 7.1 Chaordic organisations

Sometimes organisations find this a difficult challenge. For CBOs the challenge is often to work with a partner that in many ways operates contrary to core CBO values. For example, reward systems and incomes within a corporation are markedly different from those within a CBO. Many CBOs find market mechanisms distasteful even. These tensions in the Canadian forestry example led to some CBOs exiting the collaborations. For governments the challenge often involves reassigning authority. For example, in both the Madagascar and South African cases central governments had to give up traditional authority. For business, the principles require a willingness to work in a collaboration where profitability will not be the critical guiding question, and other issues such as equity will be legitimate goals. Large corporations find particularly challenging the need to co-ordinate the implications of their SLC work throughout their organisations and often even to their suppliers. For example, the implications of GRI are that a corporation will collect enormous amounts of data, which often also means creating new data-collecting systems. In the Canadian forestry case, there was the difficult issue of aligning the whole corporation—including developing new wood-harvesting techniques, gaining loggers' support and retraining them. Often this type of change takes time and CBOs have a tendency to be impatient and unfamiliar with change processes in large organisations.

Designing for mutual accountability

The SLC initiatives cannot do their learning and change work through a command system. There must be willingness to participate in a change effort in good faith. However, good faith must be supported by structures and processes of accountability.

The SLC initiatives all have co-ordinating forums, and most often these take the form of committees or, if the SLC initiative is large, new CBOs. A CBO is the preferred form because it is particularly flexible, associated with low costs, and there is usually little need for capital investment. The general guideline is to have all the key stakeholders involved in the key governance forums. Some people debate about whether they should be 'representatives' of stakeholders or simply 'participants' from collaborating organisations. A pragmatic response suggests that, as long as you have the confidence of the key stakeholders and can access the resources needed to achieve the SLC goals, either approach can work.

The planning and work forums are actually more important than the governance ones. People will support the SLC if they understand and have participated in establishing the goals, and if they find the work being done useful. The subsidiarity principle suggests that the important action is with the work and the people who are doing it. The cases organise work in various ways, depending in particular on the scale and duration of the SLC initiative.

- In the US banking case the civic government created the URA (Urban Redevelopment Authority) with members including CBOs and banks (Fig. 7.4). The URA creates CDAGs (Community Development Advisory Groups) with each bank; although most meet with their bank counterparts quarterly, the case bank CDAG meets monthly. This municipal government intervention is backed up with all of the government's tools and its influence over where government, hospitals and schools do their banking—a tool the government has made clear it will use as a carrot and stick. However, in practice the government often does not participate and the meetings are between bank and CBO representatives. Both the bank and CBOs have their own groups where they deliberate separately.

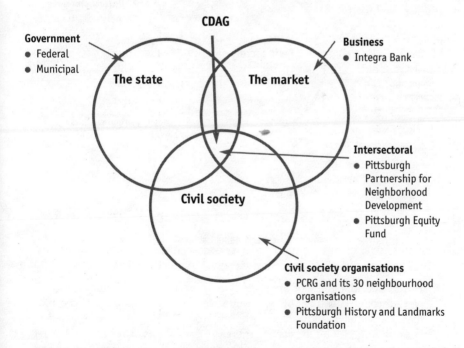

FIGURE 7.4 US banking case structure

- In India, the Centre for Technology Development and the new organisations it has founded are all CBOs with stakeholders on their boards (see Fig.
  7.5). However, there is a high degree of confidence in the pro bono senior
  retired leaders and their ability to achieve the objectives with substantial
  independence. Memoranda of understanding for particular projects are
  important tools that are developed by circulation among stakeholders for
  comment and addition until consensus is reached.

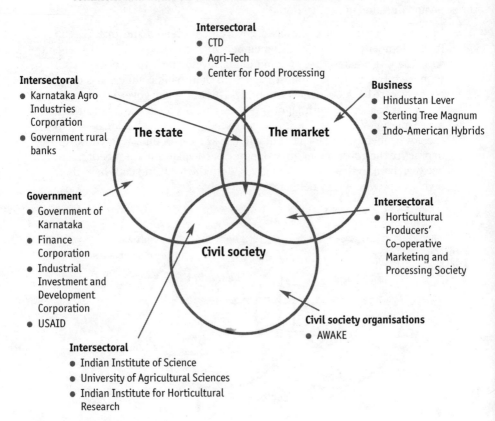

Intersectoral
- CTD
- Agri-Tech
- Center for Food Processing

Intersectoral
- Karnataka Agro
  Industries
  Corporation
- Government rural
  banks

Business
- Hindustan Lever
- Sterling Tree Magnum
- Indo-American Hybrids

The state

The market

Government
- Government of
  Karnataka
- Finance
  Corporation
- Industrial
  Investment and
  Development
  Corporation
- USAID

Intersectoral
- Horticultural
  Producers'
  Co-operative
  Marketing and
  Processing Society

Civil society

Civil society organisations
- AWAKE

Intersectoral
- Indian Institute of Science
- University of Agricultural Sciences
- Indian Institute for Horticultural
  Research

FIGURE 7.5 Indian economic development case

- During the first years of the Canadian forestry conflict, communications
  were through meetings of representatives from various parties' committees. Individuals and groups withdrew from the process and rejoined at
  various points along the way. In this case, the villages of Tofino and Ucluet
  and the First Nations people acted both as civil society organisations and
  to a lesser extent as governments (Fig. 7.6). Although they had some
  government powers which gave them status and legitimacy, these powers
  were not critical in resolving the dispute. They were actively involved in
  civil disobedience like other civil society organisations. The First Nations

were particularly powerful both because of their historic claims and because the courts recognised the legal basis for their land claims that remained unsettled. The company Iisaak is jointly owned by the First Nations and MB (now Weyerhaeuser). Several CBOs sit on the board of directors.

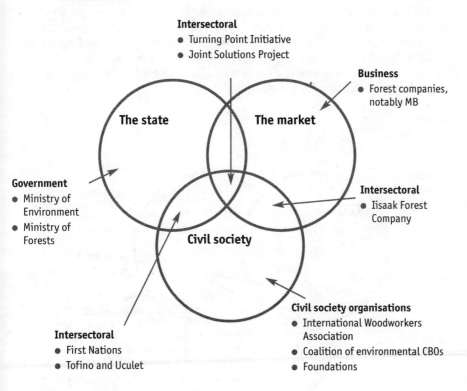

Intersectoral
- Turning Point Initiative
- Joint Solutions Project

The state

The market

Business
- Forest companies, notably MB

Government
- Ministry of Environment
- Ministry of Forests

Civil society

Intersectoral
- Iisaak Forest Company

Civil society organisations
- International Woodworkers Association
- Coalition of environmental CBOs
- Foundations

Intersectoral
- First Nations
- Tofino and Uculet

FIGURE 7.6 Canadian forestry case

A new multi-stakeholder group, the JSP (Joint Solutions Project) was created in August 2000 to act as a catalyst for change in the region. JSP members included many of the same environmental groups' leaders who had been active in Clayoquot Sound, but also have participation from a broader cross-section of forest companies. The industry and environmental caucuses struggled to clarify their own agendas before they could participate in the JSP. A separate process comprising First Nations groups called the Turning Point Initiative led to resolution of land-use issues and First Nations claims through discussions with logging and tourism companies, local governments, labour and environmental groups and the provincial government.

- In the Philippines the parties meet as needed. The farmers have seven co-operatives organised into a confederation (Fig. 7.7). This confederation, like most co-operatives, integrates both community-based principles such as 'one person, one vote', and economic objectives where the principle is 'one dollar, one vote'. The company Dolefil and/or the government agent PhilRice and/or the CBO TACDRUP sit with the confederation to discuss matters and make decisions. Any group can initiate a meeting with the other parties. The joint venture is covered by a memorandum of agreement between Dole and the farmers' co-operative organisations for the price guarantee and buy-back agreement, and agreement between Dole and TACDRUP for post-harvest services.

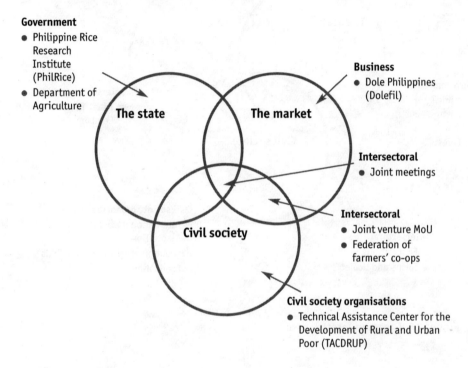

Government
- Philippine Rice Research Institute (PhilRice)
- Department of Agriculture

The state

The market

Business
- Dole Philippines (Dolefil)

Intersectoral
- Joint meetings

Intersectoral
- Joint venture MoU
- Federation of farmers' co-ops

Civil society

Civil society organisations
- Technical Assistance Center for the Development of Rural and Urban Poor (TACDRUP)

FIGURE 7.7 Philippine rice case

- AA (Amanz'abantu) in South Africa (Fig. 7.8) is unusual because it is structured as a for-profit SLC organisation. The AA structure is based on traditional construction consortia as a model. AA has its own staff and is jointly owned by the lead contractors doing the work. The staff co-ordinate the work of the contractor-owners who have legal agreements with AA to do specific parts of the project.

   AA ownership is influenced by the government's goal to include HDCs (historically disadvantaged communities—non-whites). Thirty per cent of

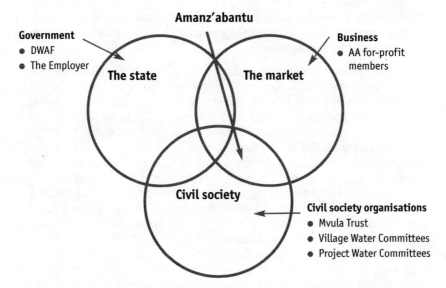

FIGURE 7.8 South African water case

AA's shares were designated and reserved for allotment to future HDCs. Each of the for-profit companies developed a partnership with an HDC. Although the original AA group offered Mvula Trust shares, the Trust declined out of concern that this profit-making role would create a conflict with its primary mission to support the voice of communities. However, to ensure the Trust had a strong role it was agreed that it would have a board member with full voice at board meetings, including a vote within the agreed board decision-making framework of agreement by consensus. Additionally, it was agreed that AA staff hired to provide ISD would be jointly hired by the Trust and AA and report to AA's managing director. The Trust led development of the local village committees that eventually became responsible for ongoing maintenance.

Relationships with the government are defined in a contract with AA. The contract is 'input' priced, with each item from a chair and office rental to an hour of engineers' time needed in a project assigned a fixed price.[1] The government identifies priorities through a planning and budgetary process, and asks AA to prepare a development proposal for individual projects. The government's role is co-ordinated by 'the Employer', an office established to both develop specific contracts within the provincial scope of work and to ensure that AA does the work as specified in the contracts. The role of the government was further complicated by its parallel activity

---

1 This proved a very unsatisfactory approach from the government's point of view, with such high profit margins for the companies that they voluntarily reduced the prices. Subsequently the contract became output-based.

to develop a new water public policy framework. This led to devolution of water authority from the national government to a new government level referred to as local government.

- The Madagascar development structure was driven by the need to create new road users' associations and by the sponsorship of USAID (the US Agency for International Development). With agreement of the national government, the Agency established the project (Fig. 7.9). It contracted with an international company, Chemonics, to lead the development. The process was managed by Chemonics, with proposals in response to the request for bids for road-building reviewed by a national committee of Chemonics and government ministry representatives, which made recommendations to another committee of government representatives and USAID. Chemonics contracted with local people to develop the road users' associations, which then became the centre for the ongoing maintenance.

  The AUPs (road users' associations) are the key SLC innovation. Social organisers emphasise the importance of letting villagers identify their own appropriate structure. The AUPs have developed with four key variables. First is size: some AUPs are based on communal boundaries, and some are subsets of them. In the case of Kalalao, the road covers three communes and there are three organisationally distinct AUPs.

  The second variable is the degree of their integration. In at least one case all the AUPs within a specific region have joined into a federation. In some instances the AUPs are organised into a federation along a specific road and have joint administration. In others, such as Kalalao, they are more loosely connected and maintain separate administrations and toll booths.

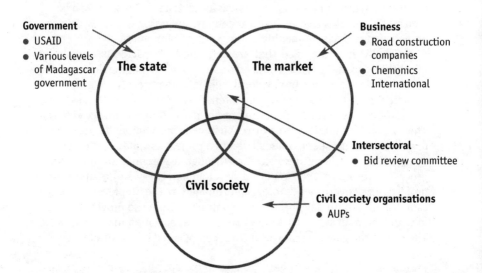

Government
- USAID
- Various levels of Madagascar government

The state

The market

Business
- Road construction companies
- Chemonics International

Intersectoral
- Bid review committee

Civil society

Civil society organisations
- AUPs

FIGURE 7.9 Madagascar road-building

The third variable is the actual financing mechanisms. In some, the communal and *sous-préfectures* make larger contributions to the AUP maintenance budgets than others. There is also variation in the amount raised through membership in the AUP and tools. Related to this is the fourth distinction, which is the degree to which the AUP is structured as a 'mass' organisation; some aim to have all adults as members, and others have more limited goals.

• The GRI structure is based on the concept of formally organised 'constituencies' or stakeholder groups. The Stakeholder Council is the formal stakeholder policy forum within the GRI structure (Fig. 7.10). It serves as an active multi-stakeholder body for debating and deliberating key strategic and policy issues facing the GRI. The Council has 60 members, comprising a balance of stakeholder and geographic constituencies. It meets twice yearly. Council members are elected at an annual meeting of the organisational stakeholders. The Council appoints board members with designated representation on the board of labour (10%), civil society activist organisations (25%), business (40%) and intermediating groups such as research organisations and professional associations (25%). UNEP and the UN's Global Compact do not participate as a 'member', but they have provided important support.

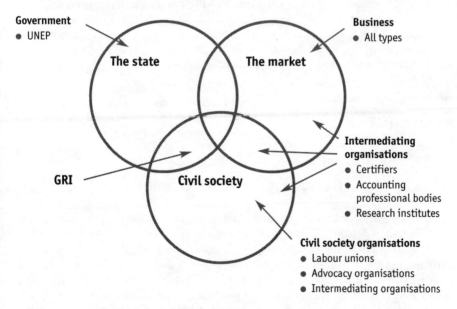

FIGURE 7.10 Global Reporting Initiative case

• TAI (The Access Initiative) and PP10 (Partnership for Principle 10), being relatively young, are still evolving. TAI is a formally constituted organisation led by a core committee comprising six CBO members, and the World

Resources Institute acts as the secretariat. PPIO is an informal organisation led by a committee of the whole. The committee is comprised of all the TAI CBOs, governments and international organisations wishing to participate, committed to the PPIO values, and willing to make commitments to improve their own performance, to contribute to the improvement of other partners' performance and to contribute to the collective work of PPIO. Structures at the national level vary to reflect particular opportunities.

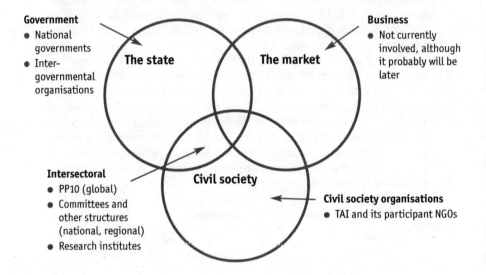

Government
- National governments
- Inter-governmental organisations

Business
- Not currently involved, although it probably will be later

Intersectoral
- PP10 (global)
- Committees and other structures (national, regional)
- Research institutes

Civil society organisations
- TAI and its participant NGOs

The state   The market   Civil society

FIGURE 7.11   TAI case

Designing for effectiveness

Structurally the SLC initiatives all can be best thought of as inter-organisational and social networks (Oliver 1990; Gulati and Gargiulo 1999; Cross and Parker 2004) and attempts to organise *under-organised* relationships (Brown 1983). For most of the participating organisations the SLC initiatives are a minor part of their work, and yet resources from all the participants are needed to achieve the SLC objective. The network form is a logical choice in such a situation, and combines benefits of relatively low costs, ability to leverage resources, operating flexibility to achieve the goals, and ease of scaling-up.

The network quality of SLC initiatives can be summarised by four points adapted from Rupert Chisholm's work on an SLC initiative (although he did not call it that).

- From a structural and analytical perspective, they operate at a level between organisations and society in general. Activities revolve around a relatively broad vision and general goals that reflect the interests of multiple organisations.

- They provide a forum where organisations can develop a broader understanding of problems and opportunities (the 'consensual knowledge'), and can take collective action based on that understanding.

- Participating organisations are loosely tied and are usually considered 'participants', or in more formal cases 'members'. They join a network based on their interest in, and ability to contribute to, a network's action, as well as some criteria established by the network. They participate within the network on a collectively defined basis that usually allows for a great variation in intensity of participation based on an organisation's desires.

- The SLC initiatives are self-regulating. Some networks have official entry and exit provisions to define who is 'inside' and who is 'outside'. However, entry and exit usually is relatively easy, and organisations may be participants without adhering to all the action activities of the network. Through participant decisions and activities SLC initiatives establish their own agenda and range of action, conditions for voice, obligations, and penalties for non-compliance (Chisholm 1998).

A network typology in Table 7.2 is another way to analyse the SLC cases. In this table networks increase in goal complexity. Each of the network types in this table must be competent in achieving the goals of the preceding network types.

All of the SLC networks are one of the two most complex: societal change or generative change. The Philippines rice and US bank cases are perhaps the classic societal change networks. Being of relatively modest scale (although products of much bigger government system changes), they can aspire to directly connect with all those who will experience SLC. These cases can be conceived as nodes within a generative change network. For example, the Philippines case might be part of a much larger strategy to reform farming and land ownership. The US bank case can be thought of as part of a national government initiative to change the relationship between the banking and community development sectors. The Indian, Canadian and Madagascar cases also fall into this category of societal change networks, although they also have impressive scaling-up objectives. The Canadian forestry case is an interesting example of an SLC initiative that started in a small geographic area and ended up changing the approach on most of the Pacific coast of Canada.

Generative change networks are challenged to develop a perspective of the whole system that they are trying to influence, and to identify critical interventions they can take to catalyse the change. GRI and TAI are the archetypical generative change networks. Aiming for global change, there is no way that they can be directly involved in the change they seek with all the organisations that have to change in order to reflect the networks' goals. Even thinking in terms of being directly responsible for achieving a 'tipping point' where the dominant paradigm shifts to reflect the concerns of TAI and GRI may be overly ambitious. Rather, they have to create and pick some particularly critical networks through which the change can spread.

To analyse SLC initiatives and networks, a typology with seven network types has been developed. The different types of networks can do different things, they require distinct skills to manage and they have distinct development processes. The core process in this typology involves a movement from generating data to information to knowledge to wisdom to action on an increasingly large scale. Listed in terms of this process from the simplest to the most complex type, these are:

1 Information network	This is most often what people think of when they think of a 'network'. Through it, participants share information about a common interest, with the onus on them to do so. It does not develop a common agenda.
2 Knowledge network	The goal is to produce new knowledge, skills and tools for those in the network. It has a defined research agenda, and participation allows sharing costs and enhancing access to data.
3 Community of practice	Participants share and develop information, knowledge, wisdom and capacity. This requires deep dialogue, open sharing and self-organised, joint-action development agendas. Benefits of participation include much more rapid development of solid and robust answers to questions of common interest.
4 Task network	When people want to undertake a specific task that requires diverse resources and co-ordination of action, they may form a network that dissolves after completion.
5 Purposeful network	Often an issue requires ongoing attention by a group of people or organisations, and they come together to co-ordinate their action and resources on an indefinite basis.
6 Societal change network	This type of network produces SLC among members who are intersectoral. The members are issue stakeholders, who undertake deep dialogue and open sharing, and collective co-ordinated and synergistic action. The change requires their collective competences and networks.
7 Generative change network	SLC is also produced by this type of network, but the goal is to generate innovation/change/action beyond *participant* boundaries. The work is done for network members and those beyond—expanding participation and influence is important. Again, it requires deep dialogue and open sharing, and collective co-ordinated and synergistic action. The work is done collaboratively because it requires collective competences and scale.

TABLE 7.2 A network typology

A critical common network competence that all SLC initiatives must develop is operating as a CP (community of practice) (Wenger 1998a; Allee 2000; Wenger and Snyder 2000). A community of practice is different from a community of interest or a geographical community, neither of which implies a shared practice. A CP defines itself along three dimensions:

- **What it is about**—it is a *joint enterprise* as understood and continually renegotiated by its members.

- **How it functions**—mutual engagement binds members together into a social entity.

- **What capability it has produced**—over time, members develop a *shared repertoire* of communal resources (routines, sensibilities, artifacts, vocabulary, styles, etc.) (Wenger 1998b)

CPs must be able to create places and processes where learning is an important activity. This does not have to be structurally complicated, but the activity has to be integrated into the routines and forums of the networks. For example, with India's Centre for Technology Development there is a very informal and open sharing process at its office. People from all the different projects have their own office, but often work around one big table where they are constantly sharing experiences and ideas. A similar atmosphere of openness pervades the meetings of the CDAG in the banking case—they are not simply agenda-driven but have space and time to explore possibilities and learn from one another. In the Canadian forestry case, the JSP's major function is as a learning community, although in the early stage it focuses on planning.

Often the learning processes are very badly done. One reason is that people equate 'action' with 'good'. Business people in particular tend to be impatient with the type of reflective processes necessary for good learning. Also, the learning is often confused with evaluation. For example, despite hundreds of millions of dollars of investment and recognition that its water projects were a big experiment, the South African government did not invest in learning. It did have an evaluation and accountability process—but this was quite different. As part of the evaluation process, the Minister and senior government officials responsible would call together people from the initiatives in a formal university lecture hall, sit at the front, pose questions and urge further action.

Structurally the cases are all remarkable in the small size in terms of staff and resources that are devoted to the co-ordinating forums. The largest is GRI with a budget of a few million dollars and a staff of about a dozen. India's CTD, arguably the most complex, has even fewer staff among the components described and a much smaller budget. As *networks,* a core task is leveraging the resources of network members rather than creating a centralising bureaucracy in the fashion of most intergovernmental secretariats. This reflects their core work is to weave together, rather than to directly do.

Perhaps the best guiding image to use in structuring an SLC initiative is the one that comes from the societal evolutionary perspective described in Chapter 2. SLC initiatives are responding to the differentiation–integration imperative. That is to say, given the increased specialisation of organisations (the differentiation aspect), the goal is to create structures that weave together the differences to address complex issues that are not addressed by uni-sectoral organisations. However, the structures must not overwhelm or control the participating organisations. If this occurs, then the organisations lose their distinctive sectoral qualities and legitimacy, and hence their value to the collaboration. This is why network organisations which can provide this type of horizontal structure and flexibility are so important for SLC initiatives.

References

Allee, V. (2000) 'Knowledge Networks and Communities of Practice', *OD Practitioner* 32.4.

Austin, J. (1998) *The Collaboration Challenge: Making the Most of Strategic Alliances between Non-profits and Corporations* (Social Enterprise Series Working Paper, Harvard Business School 6).

Austrom, D., and L. Lad (1989) 'Issues Management Alliances: New Responses, New Values, and New Logics', *Research in Corporate Social Performance and Policy* 11: 233-55.

Brown, L.D. (1983) *Managing Conflict at Organizational Interfaces* (Reading, MA: Addison-Wesley).

Carson, A.S. (2002) 'Establishing Public–Private Partnerships: Three Tests of a Good Process', *International Applied Business Research Conference*, Puerto Vallarta, Mexico.

Chisholm, R. (1998) *Developing Network Organizations: Learning From Practice and Theory* (New York: Addison-Wesley).

Council of Europe (Local and regional authorities in Europe) (1994) *Definition and Limits of the Principle of Subsidiarity* (Council of Europe, www.coe.int/T/E/Legal_Affairs/Local_and_regional_Democracy/Steering_Committee_(CDLR)/Publications/Authorities_Series/55.pdf).

Cross, R., and A. Parker (2004) *The Hidden Power of Social Networks* (Boston, MA: Harvard Business School).

Gray, B., and D. Wood (1991) 'Collaborative Alliances: Moving from Practice to Theory', *Journal of Applied Behavioral Science* 27.1: 3-22.

Gulati, R., and M. Gargiulo (1999) 'Where Do Interorganizational Networks Come From?', *The American Journal of Sociology* 104.5: 1,439-93.

Halal, W.E. (2001) 'The Collaborative Enterprise: A Stakeholder Model Uniting Profitability and Responsibility', *Journal of Corporate Citizenship* 2 (Summer 2001): 27-42.

Hock, D. (1999) *Birth of the Chaordic Organization* (San Francisco: Berrett-Koehler).

Maturana, H.R., and F.J. Varela (1998) *The Tree of Knowledge: The Biological Roots of Human Understanding* (Boston, MA: Shambhala, rev. edn).

NRC–BPD (Natural Resources Cluster–Business Partners for Development (2001) *Tri-Sector Partnerships for Managing Social Issues in the Extractive Industries: Las Cristinas Gold Mining Project, Venezuela—Health Care Partnership* (London: Natural Resources Cluster/Business Partners for Development).

Oliver, C. (1990) 'Determinants of Interorganizational Relationships: Integration and Future Direction', *Academy of Management Review* 15.2: 241-65.

Perlas, N. (2000) *Dealing with Complexity, Power and Resources: The Importance of Tri-Sector Partnerships for Advancing World Food Security* (Center for Alternative Development Initiatives, www.cadi.ph/Features/Feature_Article_3.htm).

Waddell, S. (2000) *Emerging Models for Developing Water Systems for the Rural Poor: From Contracts to Co-Production* (Research and Survey Series; London: Business Partners for Development, Water and Sanitation Cluster, www.bpd-waterandsanitation.org).

—— (2002) 'Analysis: Transforming Corporate Supply Chains into Whole Systems', *Ethical Corporation Magazine* (www.ethicalcorp.com).

Waddock, S. (1989) 'Understanding Social Partnerships: An Evolutionary Model of Partnership Organizations', *Administration and Society* 21: 78-100.

—— (1991) 'A Typology of Social Partnership Organizations', *Administration and Society* 22.4: 380-415.

—— and J. Post (1995) 'Catalytic Alliances for Social Problem Solving', *Human Relations* 48.8: 951-73.

Warner, M. (2000) 'Tri-Sector Partnerships for Social Investment within the Oil, Gas and Mining Sectors: An Analytical Framework' (Working Paper No. 2; London: Business Partners for Development, Natural Resources Cluster, CARE International; www.bpd-naturalresources.org/media/pdf/working/work2.pdf).

Wenger, E. (1998a) *Communities of Practice* (New York: Cambridge University Press).

—— (1998b) 'Communities of Practice: Learning as a Social System', *Systems Thinker*, June 1998.

—— and W.M. Snyder (2000) 'Communities of Practice: The Organizational Frontier', *Harvard Business Review*, January/February 2000: 139-45.

Wheatley, M. (1992) *Leadership and the New Science: Learning about Organizations from an Orderly Universe* (San Francisco: Berrett-Koehler).

Chapter 8
What are the SLC lessons?

The concept of 'societal learning and change' is drawn out of the cases. It is not a concept that any of the participants in the cases had in mind or even knew about. The people in the cases can be considered SLC pioneers working entrepreneurially by trial and error. They drew on diverse personal experiences, with little organisational development and design knowledge, and even less of large-systems change knowledge and skills. However, from their experiences some lessons become obvious. There is no need to repeat their errors, and these pioneers' work can guide future practitioners.

Lesson 1: Keep focused on the work— both tangible and intangible

In SLC initiatives there are two work components. One is the more traditional aspect usually associated with a relatively tangible product that directly addresses goals of 'the work'. In addition there is an intangible factor of relationship creation. For example, Amanz'abantu built the water *and* institutional infrastructure; in Madagascar people's skills in road-building *and* community organising were developed; India produced new economic activity *and* connections to both the marginalised and the academic communities; TAI created a framework and measures for participatory practice in environmental decision-making *and* a structure for bringing them to life through new CBO–government relationships. Creating the intangible relationships is the distinctive power behind SLC initiatives, but they must be built through completing more tangible outcomes.

Some people in the initiatives—typically the business people—will be more focused on the tangible. Others—typically the CBOs—will be more focused on the intangibles. This follows naturally from their core logics as discussed in Chapter 4. The trick of SLC initiatives is to integrate these so that they are both achieved, and this requires developing distinct individual and collective skills and competences.

Keeping focused on the work also means paying attention to the danger of shifting goals. This can easily occur, as an SLC initiative struggles through complexities of putting together the resources and doing the work. Bureaucratic process outcome indicators such as the number of reports completed or creation of tools and events can creep in as substitutes for good indicators of whether useful work is being done. For example, the GRI faces the danger of measuring its success in terms of the number of companies using its framework, rather than in terms of the reason for promoting use of the framework—to generate substantial improvement in terms of the environmental, economic and social impact of companies. For the US banking case, the monthly meetings might simply become ritualistic events rather than sessions that produce new community development and banking initiatives.

Lesson 2: Design a co-owned 'container' from experience

There is a common fatal trap: people begin by discussing how to organise themselves *vis-à-vis* a big vision. They get lost in theoretical discussion about how decisions should be made, the constitutions and bylaws, questions about votes, and where resources for the big goals will come from. If they hold together through these types of discussion, in the end they usually produce a structure and processes that actually inhibit useful work being done and burden people with unnecessary complexity.

The better path is to focus on the work and pay attention to the organisational relationships that best achieve the goals. SLC initiatives must create a new space where all the participants can feel ownership and responsibility. If the initiative is too attached to one participant or a subgroup, others will consider it 'their' responsibility. By collectively developing the organisational structures based on shared relationships and real experiences, the structures are more likely to be solid and co-owned.

Co-ownership means a psychological space, more than anything else. GRI was developed as a programme of the CBO CERES, but this was an administrative connection rather than an ownership one. CERES was unequivocal that its role was merely steward for development of GRI on behalf of the broader community, and decisions were made collectively.

Successful SLC initiatives reflect the well-worn organisational development adage that 'structure follows strategy', and the additional notion that structure should grow out of experience with completing valued work. TAI did not start with a comprehensively designed strategy. Rather, people experimented in developing cases and a methodology to better understand the work of giving life to participatory practice in environmental decision-making. They took an action learning approach to developing its structure by identifying the three competences needed to do the work (environmental measurement, legal processes and participatory action). When these could not be found in one organisation, the concept of national partnerships of CBOs arose. Rather than define their decision-making process at the beginning, the partners developed sufficient trust and commitment to develop the methodology and cases. As collective decisions were needed, a leadership group emerged. This group does not present itself as a 'permanent leadership group', but recognises itself to be a steward for the evolving structure.

With a work focus and concern for effectiveness, experience demonstrates that successful SLC initiatives remain small and flexible. Often they do not require any staffing, but rather simply a co-ordinating forum such as the Community Development Advisory Group with the banking example and the regular work meetings that take place as part of the Philippines case.

Lesson 3: Make experimenting, learning and teaching core

SLC initiatives are work-based learning (Raelin 1999). Experimenting, learning and teaching are core tasks, and should not be considered nice options. Success depends on them. Doing these tasks well greatly reduces costs and speeds up development by avoiding repetitive mistakes and by identifying and broadly applying lessons as quickly as possible.

SLC initiatives are fragile even after they may seem well established because they usually exist in a hostile operating environment that is still working on principles from an earlier age. Capacity-building and educating others about how these initiatives work are critical to survival.

Explicit learning strategies with community of practice capacity must be developed to reflect their role as core work. The culture and processes of the SLC initiatives must value and integrate the learning cycle of reflect–plan–act. This means (1) explicit goal-setting and task definition with (2) regular reporting and collective reviews to identify key lessons and (3) integrating them into next steps rather than just leaving them as academic lessons. Evaluations should be framed as learning processes and made a regular part of a work year.

One way to integrate this cycle is to include an academic or research group in the collaboration. Without a doubt, part of GRI's early success was its association with Tellus Institute and others that had the learning cycle as part of their core work. The same is true for TAI with the leadership of the World Resources Institute and its research partners which framed the whole initiative around development of a methodology and learning at the national and global levels.

Usually SLC participants only think of learning vis-à-vis their core substantive goal such as building roads or halting clear-cutting of forests. However, equally important are lessons and capacity development with respect to organising effectiveness. Is the SLC initiative actually functioning well as an organisation—does it adequately leverage participants' resources? Does it communicate well with its core stakeholders? Is it cost-effective? All these questions also require learning strategies, given the complex nature of SLC work.

Because SLC initiatives are complex social experiments, timing is important to get them launched and to grow them. The Philippine case arose out of an unusual constellation of factors that presented an opportunity that would have been easy to overlook. These factors included land reform, CBO knowledge about organic farming, a company learning it needed partners, and an intersectoral entrepreneur. TAI would have been much harder to organise without the World Summit on Sustainable Development as an event that provided a focus for raising the necessary money and getting the initiating tasks completed. Sometimes this timing is represented by exhaustion of other, more traditional methods. For example, in the Canadian forestry case, failure of government-led solutions was a necessary precondition.

SLC practitioners should never assume that they have 'got it' and their future is assured. With learning comes the need for teaching. Changes in ownership and individuals can turn success into failure. A new owner of the US bank wanted to tear up the agreement with the community organisations, and only concerted effort by all the other partners—including serious threats—convinced the new owner of the mutual value and importance of the relationship. A new CEO of the major forest company involved in the Canadian case raised the spectre of taking the carefully crafted SLC relationships back to square one. Until the principles behind an SLC initiative become integrated into the general operating environment, its pioneers must develop processes to initiate newcomers and teach people how they work.

Lesson 4: Recognise innovating and change as core

Innovation and deep change to create a better future are the prizes of SLC initiatives. Although these initiatives often involve first- and second-order change, their fundamental distinctive quality is their third-order change task, as Chapter 6 described. In this deep type of change, negotiation tools are inappropriate and the ability to elicit and operationalise imaginative visions is required. The type of change that is fundamental to SLC initiatives requires visioning and large system planning processes. Change is a complex field with some excellent resources (Bunker and Alban 1997; Holman and Devane 1999; Jasanoff and Wynne 1998; Kotter 2002; Senge *et al.* 1999).

Once the innovative change work of SLC initiatives is appreciated, some implications flow. For example, resistance to change must be directly addressed (see Table 8.1). People and organisations that can be classified as 'early adapters' should be sought out for SLC leadership in potential participant organisations. These are people who are interested in new ideas and have a history of championing them. A 'skunk works' strategy is often necessary. This involves establishing a safe space and permission for people from partnering organisations to experiment and explore opportunities, and develop tools, strategies and concepts so they can be mainstreamed. These show up as pilots within divisions in businesses and trial programmes in government departments and projects within CBOs.

SLC strategies can have quite dramatic change implications for participating organisations that are usually unrecognised at the beginning. The businesses involved in Amanz'abantu basically redefined their product from simple infrastructure construction to the building of sustainable water systems. In Madagascar, road construction companies had to become trainers of villagers in road construction

Resistance	Respond by
Fear of the unknown	Offering information and encouragement Visioning the future
Need for security	Clarifying intentions and methods
No felt need to change	Demonstrating the problem or opportunity while offering support
Vested interests threatened	Enlisting key people in change planning
Contrasting interpretations	Disseminating valid information and facilitating group sharing
Poor timing	Delaying change and awaiting a better time
Lack of resources	Providing supporting resources and/or reducing performance expectations

TABLE 8.1 Resistance to change and what to do

Source: Raelin 2003

and maintenance techniques. The American CBOs had to change from being critics of banks to collaborating with them, as did the environmental organisations in Canada with the forest companies. These types of shift also reflect shifts in required skills and competences.

The change work of SLC initiatives includes personal change for the participating individuals, as well as organisational change. For example, it involves changing beliefs and stereotypes and revealing limiting assumptions. The poor tend to see the wealthy as insensitive and greedy, whereas the wealthy tend to see the poor as lazy and without resources. People from developed countries tend to see those from developing countries as unsophisticated, uneducated and in need of help, whereas those from developing countries tend to see those from developed countries as imperialistic and insensitive to local values. Bankers assumed that enforcement of loans agreements required costly legal processes, and did not understand that communities could organise themselves to enforce loans in much less costly ways. As initiatives that involve changing core beliefs and assumptions, SLC initiatives' development can be accelerated by making explicit any beliefs that hinder progress and then addressing them.

SLC initiatives can spread change by creating new interpersonal networks and structures for interaction and collaboration. This is most obvious in the GRI and TAI with their explicit growing global network structure. However, in the Canadian case the networks spread the experience of one isolated region to Canada's Pacific coast. The Madagascar and CTD (India) cases have deliberate replication and expansion strategies through government and personal networks. Through the participants in the other cases the change knowledge is being disseminated less explicitly.

Change is usually associated with loss. This loss can mean moving from a tradition that evokes warmth, security and good memories into a new way of being that brings uncertainty and anxiety. Sometimes the loss can be quite unequivocal and the new way of being can make certain stakeholders worse off. In the Canadian forestry case, the loggers came out losers. For many, lower-paying tourism and service jobs replaced their high-paying logging jobs. Their loss was partly addressed through government programmes and staggering the impact through retirements and other measures. However, in the end the loss was justified by the rationale that it was inevitable, given the finite amount of forest to harvest, and that on balance the SLC strategy actually established a much better way to respond to this fact.

Recognising the role of change also means being patient. Changing mental models and building relationships of trust and mutual understanding takes time. Usually from conception to actual realisation of meaningful benefits takes a minimum of three to five years.

Lesson 5: Treat difference as an asset

The very rationale for SLC initiatives is that combining unique qualities is critical to address complex problems and realise opportunities. Although this is the rationale for most inter-organisational relationships, the differences between organisations and people participating in SLC initiatives is particularly large since they come from different organisational sectors. However, people tend to associate with others like themselves. Exploring across differences is hard work, and requires personal openness.

Participants must be willing and capable of recognising their distinct strengths and weaknesses in order to create a successful SLC initiative. This lesson highlights the importance of articulating and maintaining the differences, and creating processes to resist co-optation or merging of views. Pressure will arise that can lead one partner to become more like the other, for short-term gains. In many ways it would be much easier for Mvula Trust in South Africa to simply be another for-profit shareholder in the joint venture formed by the construction and design companies called Amanz'abantu. Mvula's unique status as a non-shareholding member of Amanz'abantu creates complications, and its role of speaking up on behalf of communities in the face of the commercial interests of the other consortium members is not easy. However, if Mvula becomes perceived by communities as being interested primarily in commercial gain, its value for Amanz'abantu will be lost.

Regular 'audits' can be undertaken as assessments of participants in terms of their sectoral assets critical for success. The tables in Chapter 4 that describe the attributes of organisations in the three sectors can be used to do these types of audits. They give a framework for assessing whether a CBO is becoming more like a business, or vice versa.

Treating difference as a serious asset has organisational implications. People from the different sectors must spend time working together and building peer relationships. In South Africa at each level in Amaz'abantu's team both institutional development (CBO) and physical infrastructure construction (business) people are included. Ironically, this was not true at the CEO level—despite good reason to believe that it was needed at least as much at that level. To recognise distinct assets, SLC initiatives require challenging long-held assumptions such as the ones behind the 'captain of the ship' model of having one person 'in charge'.

Paradox and conflict are part and parcel of treating differences as assets. If there is no tension or conflict in a collaboration, it is probably not functioning optimally. Perhaps people are only exchanging pleasantries and avoiding the real issues, or partners have slipped into safe and under-performing roles, or the wrong organisations have been brought together. The differences will create conflict as cultures and goals clash. However, challenging each other's basic assumptions and perceptions, and pressing for action that integrates seemingly conflicting goals, is the source of innovation and creativity.

Nevertheless, most people are conflict-averse. They want to be liked, and people associated with conflict are generally avoided. When conflict arises, the usual reaction is for people to shift topics, try to suppress differences or negotiate some sort of compromise. SLC initiatives require a careful recognition of minor conflicts that may be appropriately treated with these responses, and those that are critical to moving ahead and require more in-depth attention. Given the third-order change nature of SLC initiatives and their need to find transformative and innovative solutions, they require processes that allow for paradox and the development of new approaches that address diverse participants' needs.

Lesson 6: Build commitment by achieving the goals

Intersectoral relationships are not easy. They require a commitment of time, resources, mind and heart. Persistence is critical. People work at them because of both personal and organisational motivation—without both of these, success will almost certainly be elusive.

People involved in SLC initiatives usually have a strong degree of personal altruism and idealism. The senior retirees working with CTD in India continually speak of their desire for 'upliftment of the people'. The CEO of Integra bank spoke passionately about community development and the need to enhance equality. Business representatives at GRI have strong personal commitments to making the world a better place by improving corporate social, environmental and economic impacts.

However, this personal commitment must be meaningfully connected to commitment of participating organisations. Otherwise the individuals will be unable to deliver the needed resources and obtain the support for change in their organisation that are necessary to make the SLC initiative successful. This does not mean that the whole organisation must be committed to an SLC initiative for it to be successful—indeed, SLC initiatives typically are only a tiny fraction of any participating organisation's activity. However, the commitment must be strong enough to leverage the resources and generate the necessary change.

Organisational commitment is driven by a variety of motivations within the three core goals of each sector as described in Chapter 5. There must be a connection to the core goal or an initiative will probably fall short of sustained SLC. If Amanz'abantu did not produce a profit for its participating business corporations, it would not continue to participate. However, sometimes the core goals are actually quite indirect and the motivations mixed. Hindustan-Lever did not expect its participation in CTD in India to deliver financial rewards. However, it understood that its own development was being limited by attitudes towards prepared foods and the weak infrastructure—suppliers, skilled employees—for its industry. The company perceived CTD as a vehicle for popularising prepared foods and building the infrastructure.

The SLC initiatives should set quantified goals for individual participating organisations as well as the initiative as a whole. Collaborations can fall apart without constant reassessment of how the partners and the partnership are doing in terms of their distinct goals. Rather than departing dramatically, partners will usually simply drift away as they lose a sense of valued production. Ongoing self-assessment can greatly reduce this problem.

These quantifiable goals might be ones that the participating organisations monitor rather than the SLC initiative. For example, for Integra Bank a key goal was to increase its market share, and this data was regularly reviewed at the monthly meetings of the advisory group. For the Philippine case the very work of the SLC initiative provided regular feedback, since it involved providing specified quantities of high-quality rice and profit sharing.

Lesson 7: Think big—or small

Undertaking an SLC initiative might appear daunting at first, since it involves changing core dynamics in society. However, the cases illustrate that these initiatives can vary in size from that the Philippines which involves a limited and well-defined number of players to global initiatives such as GRI and TAI.

Although SLC initiatives involve basic changes to the 'rules of the game', they usually exist alongside traditional initiatives. The Philippine example did not involve changing all the rice production industry or all of Dole Foods. It was a relatively modest initiative. The American banking case is more complex and involves changes in federal banking regulation and supporting small business development and housing programmes. However, a banking initiative very similar to the case at Chicago's Shorebank took place over a decade earlier without such strong incentives and driven by individuals' skills, vision and values.

This will leave dissatisfied anyone who sees wider-scale change as a fundamental goal. SLC initiatives can be scaled up in a variety of ways. In India CTD continually creates new enterprises; in Madagascar through donor agencies new communities are being organised to take over their roads; in South Africa the government has established initiatives such as Amanz'abantu in four provinces; the Canadian case is disseminating through the participating organisations' networks; and the US banking case is spreading through bankers, regulators and community groups.

Some people start out with big dreams, as the GRI and TAI demonstrate. These are global initiatives set to change the rules of the game through dispersed, opportunistic activity. Where there are ready partners, these SLC initiatives provide a community of practice. And, in fact, they have not taken longer to initiate than smaller SLC cases. This suggests that the global truly is simply a 'different place' to do the work, rather than one that is much more complex (although the global ones are certainly more expensive!).

Lesson 8: Take a systems development perspective

SLC strategies are best approached as systems-building strategies using systems-thinking tools. A systems perspective helps clarify the complex relationships of the participants and builds an understanding of 'the whole' that is emerging at the societal systems, sector, organisation and individual levels. Often when SLC initiatives begin, all the stakeholders and their organisations are not readily apparent—even with good stakeholder analysis. Nor do all of them respond to initial attempts at engagement. Usually SLC initiatives reframe issues in novel ways, stakeholders are not organised to readily respond and often they do not recognise themselves as stakeholders.

TAI, for example, is continually learning about who in government to engage in their work to create participatory environmental decision-making. Government is not organised around that issue, but rather around traditional departmental lines. Moreover, as in most SLC cases, the issue is new. Therefore stakeholders are dispersed and part of the systems-building work for TAI actually involves organising government.

The political, economic and social systems are interdependent and deep change with respect to an issue requires understanding their relationships. What happens in one system impacts on other systems which are not organised to effectively respond to the impacts. Changing social attitudes towards old forests affected the economic system; new effective farmer CBOs and land reform provided new opportunities for companies such as Dole, but most companies simply saw land reform as a problem.

The full potential for an SLC initiative is best described from a systems perspective. Most people look at the project level, and think in terms of what their own organisation can do directly. But the SLC opportunities exist in messy and usually poorly defined arenas where organisational interests overlap and rearranging the activity of numerous stakeholders is required. Rather than think in terms of individual or organisational interests, think in terms of the latent or potential system and then steward its emergence.

Access to systems-thinking tools such network analysis and systems mapping that are so important to organisational learning is very helpful. Popularised by Peter Senge and the Society for Organisational Learning[1] (Senge 1990; Senge et al. 1994, 1999), these tools help analyse complex systems and make them manageable.

One set of these tools helps untangle complexities with eight systems archetypes that aid deepening understanding about interdependence and identifying key leverage points for action which complexity often hides. The archetypes help iden-

1   www.solonline.org

tify the source of problems. Unintended consequences are accounted for. Applying the archetype of 'Tragedy of the Commons' helps people objectively understand the systemic roles of stakeholders in environmental issues such as the Canadian forestry case. The 'Success to the Successful' archetype illuminates how to address the chronic poverty traps at the heart of the CTD, US banking and Philippines examples (Kim 1992).

Although being aware of the whole system is critical, it does not mean that the whole system should necessarily be invited in. Unengaged stakeholders can cause real problems, but sometimes they should be purposefully excluded. One good example of this is the World Health Organisation's anti-tobacco initiative, which involves some major corporations such as Novartis and Glaxo as well as CBOs. However, tobacco companies are specifically prohibited from participation as their agenda is so clearly one to prevent advancing the anti-smoking agenda.

Sometimes stakeholders do not want in or feel ambivalent. In the Canadian forestry case this dynamic was one reason that the environmental CBOs developed a porous definition about who was an active participant in their coalition. Some particular issues were so controversial that some participants had to exit for a least a period of time.

Lesson 9: Share information openly with good dialogue

This lesson is really a corollary of making learning central. Its importance makes separate mention appropriate. There were two key elements to the evolution of SLC US banking cases: the provision of information by banks that was traditionally viewed as proprietary and confidential, and successful deep dialogue across sectoral boundaries. The US federal government in the early 1970s actually tried to legislate dialogue, but that is a hard thing to do—there has to be active will. Provision of information was gradually legislated with increasing specificity, and by the late 1980s a formula evolved that required divulging lending information in sufficient detail to be useful, but still aggregated to avoid disclosure of individual identities. Without access to this information the community groups appeared to bankers—naturally enough—'to not know what they were talking about'. With these elements of information and dialogue the stakeholders were able to exchange views, challenge assumptions and develop the innovation prize of SLC initiatives.

In the Philippines the parties have sufficient trust to jointly undertake business activity that requires relatively intimate knowledge about cost structures and profitability. In South Africa, an ongoing stumbling block was the inability of the parties to share information about these types of issues openly. In fact, the companies' profits were so significant that they 'voluntarily' offered to reduce their prices in the input-based contract. Without full disclosure among the SLC participants and a way to reach agreement on fair rates of profitability, trust remained a critical issue.

For the Madagascar road-building associations, transparency and sharing of information is a key foundation of their work. CTD in India creates multi-party enterprises where information-sharing and dialogue to develop new approaches are key. A breakthrough in the Canadian forestry example was the ability of the parties to actually talk about the economics and feasibility of new approaches to forestry by creating a jointly owned forest company.

The GRI and TAI are perhaps the best examples where sharing of information and good dialogue are critical. Indeed, the whole success of these initiatives depends on it and is directed to developing it! The future of the GRI is closely tied to integrating the dialogue and information-sharing elements, not just to develop a global reporting framework but to apply it at the local enterprise level—the level where the innovation prize will be developed.

References

Bunker, B., and B. Alban (1997) *Large Group Interventions: Engaging the Whole System for Rapid Change* (San Francisco: Jossey-Bass).

Holman, P., and T. Devane (1999) *The Change Handbook: Group Methods for Shaping the Future* (San Francisco: Berrett-Koehler).

Jasanoff, S., and B. Wynne (1998) 'Science and Decisionmaking', in S.R. and E.L. Malone (eds.), *Human Choice and Climate Change* (Washington, DC: Battelle Press): 1-87.

Kim, D. (1992) *The Toolbox Reprint Series: Systems Archetypes I* (Waltham, MA: Pegasus Communications).

Kotter, J. (2002) *The Heart of Change: Real-Life Stories of How People Change their Organizations* (Boston, MA: Harvard Business School Press).

Raelin, J.A. (1999) *Work-Based Learning: The New Frontier of Management Development* (Englewood Cliffs, NJ: Addison-Wesley/Prentice Hall).

Raelin, J. (2003) 'Resistance to Change and What to Do', in *Leadership for Change Module V Materials* (Boston, MA: Boston College).

Senge, P.M. (1990) *The Fifth Discipline: The Art and Practice of the Learning Organization* (New York: Doubleday).

——, R. Ross, B. Smith, C. Roberts and A. Kleiner (1994) *The Fifth Discipline Fieldbook* (New York: Currency Doubleday).

——, A. Kleiner, C. Roberts, R. Ross, G. Roth and B. Smith (1999) *The Dance of Change: The Challenges to Sustaining Momentum in Learning Organizations* (New York: Currency Doubleday).

Chapter 9
SLC: a growth industry

Complex issues such as sustainability and globalisation are rapidly growing in importance. SLC holds promise for addressing such complex issues. The choice is not whether to undertake more SLC actions, but rather how to do so as effectively as possible. This book aims to make a contribution to that effort, but much more is needed.

In general, responses to sustainability and globalisation have been simplistic. Only recently in Northern or developed countries has sustainability begun to include social issues such as equity, and only recently in many developing countries has it begun to seriously include environmental issues. We are still at early stages of broadening economic globalisation to include social and political globalisation as well—there are few meaningful discussions let alone strategies for addressing global inequities and power structures.

Sustainability and globalisation are challenges to the fundamental way that we act, think and feel in the world. Too often environmental concerns are pitted against the economy, reflection against action, one nation against another, the haves against the have-nots, global against local; material wealth is promoted as the source of happiness, and vast inequities in life opportunities are justified. Increasingly this vision of the world is coming into conflict with the need to take a whole-systems view and act responsibly for the future of the planet. In a world of intensifying global communication and environmental interdependence, in Kuhn's terminology the contradictions are becoming more obvious and the pressure for a paradigm shift is increasing. In the terms of evolutionary sociology, in the face of increasing differentiation we need to find better mechanisms for integration.

Certainly SLC strategies are not the complete answer to these challenges, but they can make a significant contribution to addressing them. They help define the emerging paradigm and the change processes to realise that paradigm. These strategies suggest four emerging organising principles and two new systems.

The four emerging organising principles

1 Death is natural

The word 'death' is used for dramatic impact, although the word 'change' might also be used. We have to create new processes, social norms and etiquettes for letting go

of habits and traditions that are self-destructive. The concept of 'nation' was important historically, but it is hindering development of global citizenship. Environmentally destructive consumption patterns that focus on physical goods and lifestyles
that increase commuting and decrease time with children need to halt in response
to the principle of development. Rather than continue the fiction that the nuclear
family is the only or even best way to organise child-raising, we have to actively
develop alternatives. We must share the world's wealth and resources more equitably.

This is perhaps the most difficult principle, since it means changing individual
and organisational behaviours that we are accustomed to and like, and challenging
basic assumptions which can be very uncomfortable. However, the cases reveal
several traditions that are dying (see Table 9.1). In the American and Canadian
cases, perhaps the most difficult death was that of stereotypes about people in
business and CBOs, and the challenge was to move from shouting at one another to
actually listening and working together. The latter shifts are also core to the
Philippines example, the GRI and TAI. In many of the cases, notably South Africa,
India and Madagascar, the governments' mental model of control over the other
sectors had to die to make room for the collaborations.

These deaths represent shifts away from us-versus-them, linear, hierarchical and
brute power-driven ways of interacting. People found negotiations-based strategies
and separation (atomistic approaches) as barriers to developing innovation and
opportunity.

What is dying	What is developing
Atomistic (reductionist) as *the* approach	(Whole) systems thinking
Linear and mechanical mental models	Circular and biological mental models
Inter-national structures	Glocal
Negotiations as deep change	Collaboration for deep change
Hierarchy as dominant	Hierarchy embedded in networks
Power as brute force	Power as knowledge/education/information

TABLE 9.1 What is dying and what is developing?

2 Development is good

This principle paraphrases the principle 'growth is good' of William McDonough,
the University of Virginia architect who is famous for his environmental designs.
This came as a challenge to many environmentalist fans of McDonough. His point
is that growth of a child and growth of a tree are good things, and that the 'no-
growth' rhetoric of many environmentalists is a non-starter.

However, the Brundtland Commission settled on the phrase 'sustainable development' rather than 'sustainable growth' for good reason. The emerging principle

reflects the need to shift from 'growth' with its connotation of 'bigger and more is better' to a more holistic view about dimensions of our future. We need the qualitative trajectory that comes with 'development'. For example, this includes increased creativity, capacity for reflection, spiritual depth and intellectual broadening.

We can see examples of this development approach in all the cases. The American banking case focuses on integrated social–economic–political inner-city neighbourhoods development—which does not involve destruction of new lands or long commutes, as does suburbia. The Indian economic development case is grounded in creating agricultural products and activity specifically appropriate for that climate in ways that engage a cross-section of community. The Philippine case emphasises shifting to organic rice production and redefining distribution of benefits. In South Africa the case focuses on sustainable water systems in contrast to traditional approaches, as does the Madagascar case with respect to roads. The American, Indian, South African, Philippine and Madagascar cases also all focus on low-income communities and enhancing their life opportunities. The Canadian forestry example does not conclude with an end to forest harvesting, but rather reshapes it into more sustainable approaches that incorporate traditional First Nations' wisdom. Reshaping our economic growth-driven models to encompass environmental and social development is at the heart of GRI. And the essence of TAI is development of new participatory processes that will draw in more people to produce more creative responses to activities with high environmental impact.

These changes are third-order. They represent a shift to holistic, systems thinking and collaborative relationships driven by the power of new knowledge. The GRI case in particular represents a reformulation of the role of the nation-state in international affairs, but in all the cases the role of government changed significantly from being 'in control' to sharing responsibility.

3 Interdependence is critical

Profound appreciation of our world as a product of all our interactions is part and parcel of SLC initiatives. This requires shifting from heroic leadership models and individual entitlement. We must enhance our awareness of the connections between one person's success and another's actions. We must shift from thinking in terms of simplistic cause-and-effect and root causes, to become systems thinkers perceiving a multitude of influences and feedback loops.

This might also be called the complexity principle. Simplistic cause-and-effect models are attractive because they make us feel in control. However, this is very often just an illusion, as we learn when unintended consequences come back to bite us. Harvesting forests without regard to long-term impacts is straightforward—but unsustainable. For multinational companies, working with small rice farmers rather than plantations adds complexity and reduces the level of direct control—but the triple-bottom-line results can be much better. Development of water systems was much simpler with the government-only and government–business development models. However, the product is water systems that were not sustainable if people are not capable of supporting their maintenance. Complexity cannot be an excuse for throwing up our hands—it must be a force for both increasing our humbleness and further developing our ways of handling complexity.

4 Relationships are based on mutual respect

Mutual respect is a critical ingredient in third-order change and SLC initiatives. Unequal power is common, but if relationships are a function of unequal power, the innovative potential of initiatives will never be realised. Threats and power plays can only go so far. Human potential is revealed through inspiration, visions and aspirations.

This principle also means honouring diversity. This includes both the natural environment and cultural diversity as with our relationships with one another. Respect is a key driver for mutual understanding and good dialogue. The death principle suggests that indeed some cultural habits will have to change, but this does not mean that we must become less diverse. Today the rush is in favour of international homogenisation in contrast to 'development' which responds to local differences and values.

With respect comes values such as transparency, participation, accountability and subsidiarity. All of the cases responded to local, latent but under-developed potential by sharing information openly, creating participatory processes, developing mutual accountability and sharing control with local participants. The Canadian forestry case, for example, engages the First Nations people and loggers, as well as the international environmental CBOs and large forest companies. (The new forestry company owned by First Nations and MacMillan Bloedel is named Iisaak, which means 'respect' in the Nuu-Chah-Nulth language.) Open sharing of information was critical in the US banking case, which led to much more influence on a large bank by local communities. New participative processes for development of information through multi-stakeholder processes of accountability are central to GRI and TAI. One benefit from the Madagascar case when local villagers were treated as partners in road development was a substantial decrease in corruption due to transparency and accountability. The Philippine rice example required open sharing of information about profits, and the lack of such open sharing proved a stumbling block in the South African development.

The two newly emerging systems

In the diagram of the sectors as overlapping circles (Fig. 4.1), the area of SLC activity is in the overlapping parts. In this area a reconfiguration of relationships—the paradigm shift—can be seen both at the individual and organisational levels.

1 A human development system that reflects equity, honours diversity and grows
  extraordinarily productive and happy people

Creating spaces where people can express their highest aspirations is an SLC activity. Rather than focus on what is 'proper' with respect to some traditional values, or what is most economically remunerative, or what was most politically feasible, the SLC initiatives are developing innovative relationships among people to support people's broader human development.

Perhaps this is best captured in the Indian case where the senior retired people leading the initiative speak about the 'upliftment of the people' as their core objective. Rather than see the goal in simplistic economic development terms such as raising per capita income, they think of the goal as the development of happier human beings whose role in society is enhanced more broadly. We can see in the Philippine case that people transform from being potential employees in a global production system, to having more peer-like relationships that include making decisions about what they will grow and how, as well as increasing their income. In the South African and Madagascar cases, people shift from being treated as passive clients of a central government to being active participants and owners of their futures. The US banking case means traditionally marginalised people now have better access to relationships and resources necessary to further develop them-selves. Both GRI and TAI are creating new ways for people to influence the way major companies impact their lives on an array of concerns.

Many people despair at the decline in participation in traditional political elec-tions. However, these cases suggest that people are finding new ways to develop themselves and their opportunities. In the Canadian forestry case people are learn-ing new skills to communicate across traditional divides. As in the other cases, they have created new forums where they can participate in the development of their aspirational futures.

In this model, the concept of heroic leadership is replaced by one of *leaderfulness*. This model:

> does not merely present a consultative model wherein leaders in author-ity allow 'followers' to participate in their leadership. Nor does it equate to stewardship approaches that see the leader step aside to allow others to take over when necessary. Instead, it offers a true mutual model that transforms leadership from an individual property into a new paradigm that redefines leadership as a collective practice (Raelin 2003).

SLC requires everyone to act as a leader.

2 A co-production system of environmentalists, business, community and
  government

Karl Marx wrote about the 'economic superstructure' to describe the way our civilisation is driven mainly by concerns of the economic system. This is the domi-nant system in the US and more broadly in Western materialistic cultures. In response, communists created societies driven by concerns of the political system. This approach largely collapsed with the end of the Soviet Union, it is rapidly changing in China and outposts remain in Cuba and North Korea.

The SLC initiatives suggest that both of these models are faulty, and that we are developing a superstructure that integrates the three sectors of business, government and civil society. The organisations in the three sectors will not disappear—they will continue to be important. But the new 'governance' structure will be intersectoral and the organisations in the three sectors will be caught in a spider web of intersectoral relationships and they will be accountable to them.

In the traditional production model a company develops, markets and distributes its products by itself. Objections from consumers and government regulators might arise, but they would be external to the company-controlled processes. The cases suggest that a much more holistic, integrated production model is developing. In the Canadian case, this is literally seen with First Nations peoples' and MacMillan Bloedel forest company's joint ownership of the new forest company Iisaak, designed to achieve their diverse objectives. The Joint Solutions Project in the Canadian case is a new organisation for all stakeholders to produce a larger system that will meet all their objectives.

All the intersectoral spaces created in the cases are examples of this new governance production system. In the banking case, the CDAG is creating and delivering new products and services; in the Philippines case it is the joint company–cooperative committee; in the Indian case the intersectoral CBOs are creating new companies and relationships to uplift the people; Amanz'abantu in South Africa is a CBO–business consortium contracting with government to produce sustainable water systems; GRI is business and civil society organisations producing a new standards reporting structure as a macro framework to develop new relationships and triple-bottom-line action; TAI is creating joint government–CBO relationships to produce new environmental impact processes.

Given the rise of the environmental imperative in the way we organise ourselves, it is appropriate that a biological metaphor is increasingly used to describe our organisational structures (Benyus 2002; Hawken et al. 1999; Maturana and Varela 1998). This contrasts with the physics-based models of the industrial age. In this new metaphor people speak of organisations' DNA rather than their lines of authority; networks and full feedback systems are the dominant visual images rather than mechanistic linear and hierarchical production models; the focus is on 'life' rather than 'things'.

In this SLC model, becoming overwhelmed by complexity of issues is easy. However, we are only limited by our imaginations and will. The cases demonstrate the possibility and power of integrating social and technical innovation. When issues or opportunities involve business–government–civil society collaboration, the SLC framework helps clarify strategies and guide decisions more effectively.

The SLC framework emphasises that the opportunity or problem is the appropriate reference point in a collaboration, not an organisation, community or government agency. This produces a very different development path than approaches based on an organisation or community. Corporate citizenship and corporate social responsibility place the corporation in a privileged position with a corporate-centric stakeholder model. Traditional public policy models place government in charge as the one to create the needed change. And community development models typically place community organisations in a privileged position of knowing the answers and being the primary agent for change.

An SLC approach emphasises the importance of identifying how individual organisations participating in a collaboration will derive value in the collaboration at an operational level. But SLC also says there is a higher-level opportunity that is the context for assessing options and actions of a collaboration. Both sets of outcomes must be managed.

The SLC framework is helpful for collaborations because it provides the appropriate definition of the depth of the change involved. The deep, third-order change implicit with SLC can be successfully developed in a guided manner, but it requires understanding of societal structures and the change challenge. SLC as a framework helps define the skills that are needed, the time periods required, and the need to orchestrate individual, organisational, sectoral and societal change. Societies all have their own DNAs, and to respond to today's opportunities and create environment, economic, social and political success requires changing those DNAs. Through SLC strategies people are doing this.

References

Benyus, J.M. (2002) *Biomimicry: Innovation Inspired by Nature* (New York: Perennial).

Hawken, P., A. Lovins and L.H. Lovins (1999) *Natural Capitalism* (Boston, MA: Little, Brown & Co.).

Maturana, H.R., and F.J. Varela (1998) *The Tree of Knowledge: The Biological Roots of Human Understanding* (Boston, MA: Shambhala, rev. edn).

Raelin, J. (2003) *Creating Leaderful Organizations: How to Bring out Leadership in Everyone* (San Francisco: Berrett-Koehler).

Abbreviations

AA	Amanz'abantu
ACODE	Advocates' Coalition for Development and Environment
AIDS	acquired immuno-deficiency syndrome
AUP	Association Usagers de Pistes (Madagascar)
AWAKE	Association of Women Entrepreneurs of Karnataka (India)
BOTT	build–operate–train–transfer
CBO	community-based organisation
CC	corporate citizenship
CDAG	Community Development Advisory Group (USA)
CEO	chief executive officer
CERES	Coalition for Environmentally Responsible Economies
CFP	Centre for Food Processing (India)
CP	community of practice
CRA	Community Reinvestment Act (USA)
CSD	Commission for Sustainable Development (UN)
CSR	corporate social responsibility
CTD	Centre for Technology Development (India)
DWAF	Department of Water Affairs and Forestry (South Africa)
EMLA	Environmental Management and Law Association (Hungary)
ENGO	environmental NGO
GNP	gross national product
GRI	Global Reporting Initiative
HDC	historically disadvantaged community
HIV	human immunodeficiency virus
HOPCOMS	Horticultural Producers' Co-operative Marketing and Processing Society (India)
IISc	Institute of Sciences (India)
ISD	institutional and social development
ISO	International Organisation for Standardisation
IUCN	International Union for the Conservation of Nature (the World Conservation Union)
JSP	Joint Solutions Project
MB	MacMillan Bloedel
MoU	memorandum of understanding
MSP	multi-stakeholder process
NGO	non-governmental organisation
O&M	operations and management
PCRG	Pittsburgh Community Reinvestment Coalition
PEF	Pittsburgh Equity Fund

PH&L	Pittsburgh History and Landmarks Foundation
PP10	Partnership for Principle 10
PPND	Pittsburgh Partnership for Neighborhood Development
PSC	project steering committee
R&D	research and development
RfP	request for proposals
SLC	societal learning and change
TACDRUP	Technical Assistance Center for the Development of Rural and Urban Poor (Philippines)
TAI	The Access Initiative
UN	United Nations
UNDP	United Nations Development Programme
UNEP	United Nations Environment Programme
URA	Urban Redevelopment Authority (USA)
USAID	United States Agency for International Development
VP	vice-president
VWC	village water committee (South Africa)
WRI	World Resources Institute
WSSD	World Summit on Sustainable Development

Index